A Collection of Magical Writings, Fiction, Poetry and Essays

By Aleister Crowley

Copyright © 2019 Lamp of Trismegistus. All rights reserved. No part of this publication may be reproduced or transmitted in any form or by any means, electronic or mechanical, including photocopying, recording, or by any information storage and retrieval system, without permission in writing from Lamp of Trismegistus. Reviewers may quote brief passages.

ISBN: 978-1-63118-424-6

Esoteric Classics

Other Books in this Series and Related Titles

Thirty-One Hymns to the Star Goddess by Frater Achad
(978-1-63118-422-2)

Magical Essays and Instructions by Florence Farr
(978-1-63118-418-5)

Ancient Mysteries and Secret Societies by Manly P. Hall
(978-1-63118-410-9)

The First and Second Gospels of the Infancy of Jesus Christ
by Thomas and James (978-1-63118-415-4)

The Human Aura: Astral Colors and Thought Forms
by Swami Panchadasi and William Walker Atkinson
(978-1-63118-419-2)

The Book of the Watchers by Enoch (978-1-63118-416-1)

The Smoky God or A Voyage to the Inner World
by Willis George Emerson (978-1-63118-423-9)

Occult Symbolism of Animals, Insects, Reptiles, Fish and Birds
by Manly P. Hall (978-1-63118-420-8)

Rosa Alchemica, The Tables of Law & The Adoration of the Magi
by William Butler Yeats (978-1-63118-421-5)

A Collection of Writings Related to Occult, Esoteric, Rosicrucian and Hermetic Literature, Including Freemasonry, the Kabbalah, the Tarot, Alchemy and Theosophy various authors *Volumes 1-4*
(978-1-63118-713-1) (978-1-63118-714-8)
(978-1-63118-715-5) (978-1-63118-716-2)

Audio Versions are also Available on Audible and iTunes

Table of Contents

Introduction…7

The Message of the Master Therion…9

The Glow Worm…13

The Stratagem…15

The Magick Cup…33

Liber Resh…43

The Sabbath…47

The Cry of the 12th AEthyr, which is Called LOE…53

Absinthe: The Green Goddess…59

Liber Porta Lucis…79

Apollo Bestows the Violin…83

The Soul of the Desert…91

The Opium-Smoker…105

Baphomet…111

The Drug…113

Liber A'ash…125

The Dangers of Mysticism…129

The Rosicrucian…135

The Law of Liberty…139

Introduction

The word "esoteric" can be difficult to define. Esotericism in general can be seen less as a system of beliefs and more as a category, which encompasses numerous, different systems of beliefs. It's a bit of juxtaposition, since the word "esoteric" indicates something that few people know about, while the term itself broadly covers numerous philosophies, practices, areas of study and belief systems.

In a greater sense, Esotericism acts as a storehouse for secret knowledge, which is often considered ancient (by *tradition, if not by fact)*, passed down from generation to generation, in private. At various times in history, simply possessing the knowledge of some of these subjects, was considered illegal and a jailable offence, if discovered. This usually included such general topics as Alchemy, Qabalah, Hermeticism, Occultism, Ceremonial Magic, Astrology, Divination, Rosicrucianism and so on. Collectively, these areas of study were often referred to as the esoteric sciences.

Sometimes, the outer garment of a subject isn't esoteric, while what is hidden beneath it, is. As an example, Freemasonry isn't necessarily esoteric by nature (at *least not anymore),* but certain signs, passwords and handshakes given to the candidate during their initiation, are in fact, esoteric, in the sense that they are hidden from the general public.

Today, in the twenty-first century, such topics are readily available at bookstores across the country, and numerous mainsteam publishers offer beginners guides and coffee-table volumes on many of these subjects, intended for mass appeal. Books like *"The Secret"* have turned previously arcane topics into household knowledge. All that being the case, however, it isn't to say that there still aren't buried secrets to uncover, ancient wisdom being ignored and forgotten mysteries to be explored. In fact, it is often that we are only able to further our own studies by standing on the shoulders of these disappearing giants.

Lamp of Trismegistus is doing its part to help preserve humanity's esoteric history by making some of these classics available to those students who are seeking to unearth the knowledge of these ancient colossi.

So, be sure to check other titles from our *Esoteric Classics* series, as well as our *Occult Fiction*, *Theosophical Classics*, *Foundations of Freemasonry* and our *Christian Apocrypha Series*.

The Message of the Master Therion

"Do what thou wilt shall be the whole of the Law."
"There is no law beyond Do what thou wilt."
"The word of the Law is Thelema."
Thelema—means Will.

The Key to this Message is this word—Will. The first obvious meaning of this Law is confirmed by antithesis; *"The Word of Sin is Restriction."*

Again: *"... thou hast no right but to do thy will. Do that, and no other shall say nay. For pure will, unassuaged of purpose, delivered from the lust of result, is every way perfect."*

Take this carefully; it seems to imply a theory that if every man and every woman did his and her will—the true Will—there would be no clashing. *"Every man and every woman is a star"*, and each star moves in an appointed path without interference. There is plenty of room for all; it is only disorder that creates confusion.

From these considerations it should be clear that *"Do what thou wilt"* does not mean "Do what you like." It is the apotheosis of Freedom; but it is also the strictest possible bond.

Do what thou wilt—then do nothing else. Let nothing deflect thee from that austere and holy task. Liberty is absolute to do thy will; but seek to do any other thing whatever, and instantly obstacles must arise. Every act that is not in definite course of that one orbit is erratic, an hindrance. Will must not be two, but one.

Note further that this will is not only to be pure, that is, single, as explained above, but also *"unassuaged of purpose"*. This strange phrase must give us pause. It may mean that any purpose in the will would damp it; clearly, the *"lust of result"* is a thing from which it must be delivered.

But the phrase may also be interpreted as if it read "with purpose unassuaged"—i.e. with tireless energy. The conception is, therefore, of an eternal motion, infinite and unalterable. It is Nirvana, only dynamic instead of static—and this comes to the same thing in the end.

The obvious practical task of the magician is then to discover what his will really is, so that he may do it in this manner, and he can best accomplish this by the practices of *Liber Thisharb* or such others as may from one time to another be appointed.

It should now be perfectly simple for everybody to understand the Message of the Master Therion.

Thou must (1) Find out what is thy Will, (2) Do that Will with (a) one-pointedness, (b) detachment, (c) peace.

Then, and then only, art thou in harmony with the Movement of Things, thy will part of, and therefore equal to, the Will of God. And since the will is but the dynamic aspect of the self, and since two different selves could not possess identical wills; then, if thy will be God's will, Thou art That.

There is but one other word to explain. Elsewhere it is written—surely for our great comfort—"*Love is the law, love under will.*"

This is to be taken as meaning that while Will is the Law, the nature of that Will is Love. But this Love is as it were a by-product of that Will; it does not contradict or supersede that Will; and if apparent contradiction should arise in any crisis, it is the Will that can guide us aright. Lo, while in the *Book of the Law* is much Love, there is no word of Sentimentality. Hate itself is almost like Love! Fighting most certainly is Love! "*As brothers fight ye!*" All the manly races of the world understand this. The Love of *Liber Legis* is always bold, virile, even orgiastic. There is delicacy, but it is the delicacy of strength. Mighty and terrible and glorious as it is, however, it is but the pennon upon the sacred lance of Will, the damascened inscription upon the swords of the Knight-Monks of Thelema.

Love is the law, love under will.

The Glow-Worm

Concerning the Holy Three-in-Naught.

Nuit, Hadit, Ra-Hoor-Khuit, are only to be understood by the Master of the Temple.

They are above The Abyss, and contain all contradiction in themselves.

Below them is a seeming duality of Chaos and Babalon; these are called Father and Mother, but it is not so. They are called Brother and Sister, but it is not so. They are called Husband and Wife, but it is not so.

The reflection of All is Pan: the Night of Pan is the Annihilation of the All.

Cast down through The Abyss is the Light, the Rosy Cross, the rapture of Union that destroys, that is The Way. The Rosy Cross is the Ambassador of Pan.

How infinite is the distance from This to That! Yet All is Here and Now. Nor is there any There or Then; for all that is, what is it but a manifestation, that is, a part, that is, a falsehood, of THAT which is not?

Yet THAT which is not neither is nor is not That which is!

Identity is perfect; therefore the Law of Identity is but a lie. For there is no subject, and there is no predicate; nor is there the contradictory of either of these things.

Holy, Holy, Holy are these Truths that I utter, knowing them to be but falsehoods, broken mirrors, troubled waters; hide me, O our Lady, in Thy Womb! for I may not endure the rapture.

In this utterance of falsehood upon falsehood, whose contradictories are also false, it seems as if That which I uttered not were true.

Blessed, unutterably blessed, is this last of the illusions; let me play the man, and thrust it from me! Amen.

The Stratagem

The fellow-travellers climbed down on to the fiery sand of the platform. It was a junction, a junction of that kind where there is no town for miles, and where the resources of the railway and its neighbourhood compare unfavourably with those of the average quarantine station.

The first to descend was a man unmistakably English. He was complaining of the management even while he extracted his hand-baggage from the carriage with the assistance of his companion. "It is positively a disgrace to civilisation," he was saying, "that there should be no connection at such a station as this, an important station, sir, let me tell you, the pivot—if I may use the metaphor—of the branch which serves practically the whole of Muckshire south of the Tream. And we have certainly one hour to wait, and Heaven knows it's more likely to be two, and perhaps three. And, of course, there's not as much as a bar nearer than Fatloam; and if we got there we should positive and actual disgrace to the railway that allows it, to the country that tolerates it, to the civilisation that permits that such things should be. The same thing happened to me here last year, sir, though luckily on that occasion I had but half-an-hour to wait. But I wrote to *The Times* a strong half-column letter on the subject, and I'm damned if they didn't refuse to print it. Of course, our independent press, etc.; I might have known. I tell you, sir, this country is run by a ring, a dirty ring, a gang of Jews,

Scotchmen, Irish, Welsh—where's the good old jolly True Blue Englishman? In the cart, sir, in the cart."

The train gave a convulsive backward jerk, and lumbered off in imitation of the solitary porter who, stationed opposite the guard's van, had witnessed without emotion the hurling forth of two trunks like rocks from a volcano, and after a moment's contemplation had, with screwed mouth, mooched along the platform to his grub, which he would find in an isolated cottage some three hundred *yards* away.

In strong contrast to the Englishman, with his moustache afforesting a whitish face, marked with deep red rings on neck and forehead, his impending paunchiness and his full suit of armour, was the small, active man with the pointed beard whom fate had thrown first into the same compartment, and then into the same hour of exile from all their fellows.

His eyes were astonishingly black and fierce; his beard was grizzled and his face heavily lined and obviously burnt by tropical suns; but that face also expressed intelligence, strength, and resourcefulness in a degree which would have made him an ideal comrade in a forlorn hope, or the defense of a desperate village. Across the back of his left hand was a thick and heavy scar. In spite of all this, he was dressed with singular neatness and correctness; which circumstance, although his English was purer than that of his companion in distress, made the latter secretly incline to suspect him of being a Frenchman. In spite of the quietness of his dress and the self-possession of his demeanour, the sombre glitter of those black eyes, pin-points below shaggy eye-brows, inspired the large man with a certain uneasiness. Not at all a chap to quarrel with, was his thought. However, being himself a widely-travelled man—Boulogne, Dieppe, Paris, Switzerland, and even Venice—he had none of that insularity of which foreigners accuse some Englishmen, and he had endeavoured to make conversation during the journey. The small man had proved a poor companion, taciturn to a fault, sparing of words where a nod would satisfy the obligations of courtesy, and seemingly fonder of his pipe than of his fellow-man. A man with a secret, thought the Englishman.

The train had jolted out of the station and the porter had faded from the landscape. "A deserted spot," remarked the Englishman, whose name was Bevan, "especially in such fearful heat. Really, in the summer of 1911, it was hardly as bad. Do you know, I remember once at Boulogne" He broke off sharply, for the brown man, sticking the ferrule of his stick repeatedly in the sand, and knotting his brows came suddenly to a decision. "What do you know of heat?" he cried, fixing Bevan with the intensity of a demon. "What do you know of desolation?" Taken aback, as well he might be, Bevan was at a loss to reply. "Stay," cried the other. "What if I told you my story? There is no one here but ourselves." He glared menacingly at Bevan, seemed to seek to read his soul. "Are you a man to be trusted?" he barked, and broke off short.

At another time Bevan would most certainly have declined to become the confidant of a stranger; but here the solitude, the heat, not a little boredom induced by the previous manner of his companion, and even a certain mistrust of how he might take a refusal, combined to elicit a favourable reply.

Stately as an oak, Bevan answered, "I was born an English gentleman, and I trust that I have never done anything to derogate from that estate." "I am a Justice of the Peace," he added after a momentary pause.

"I knew it," cried the other excitedly. "The trained legal mind is that of all others which will appreciate my story. Swear, then," he went on with sudden gravity, "swear that you will never whisper to any living soul the smallest word of what I am about to tell you. Swear by the soul of your dead mother."

"My mother is alive," returned Bevan.

"I knew it," exclaimed his companion, a great and strange look of god-like pity illuminating his sunburnt face. It was such a look as one sees upon many statues of Buddha, a look of divine, of impersonal compassion.

"Then swear by the Lord Chancellor."

Bevan was more than ever persuaded that the stranger was a Frenchman. However, he readily gave the required promise.

"My name," said the other, "is Duguesclin. Does that tell you my story?" he asked impressively. "Does that convey anything to your mind?"

"Nothing at all."

"I knew it," said the man from the tropics. "Then I must tell you all. In my veins boils the fiery blood of the greatest of the French warriors, and my mother was the lineal descendant of the Maid of Saragossa."

Bevan was startled, and showed it.

"After the siege, sir, she was honourably married to a nobleman," snapped Duguesclin. "Do you think a man of my ancestry will permit a stranger to lift the shadow of an eyebrow against the memory of my great-grandmother?"

The Englishman protested that nothing had been further from his thoughts.

"I suppose so," proceeded the other more quietly. "And the more, perhaps, that I am a convicted murderer."

Bevan was now fairly alarmed.

"I am proud of it," continued Duguesclin. "At the age of twenty-five my blood was more fiery than it is today. I married. Four years later I found my wife in the embraces of a neighbour. I slew him. I slew her. I slew our three children, for vipers breed only vipers. I slew the servants; they were accomplices of the adultery, or if not, they should at any rate not witness their master's shame. I slew the gendarmes who came to take me—servile hirelings of a corrupt republic. I set my castle on fire, determined to perish in the ruins. Unfortunately, a piece of masonry, falling, struck me on the arm. My rifle dropped. The accident was seen, and I was rescued by the firemen. I determined to live; it was my duty to my ancestors to continue the family of which I was the sole direct scion. It is in search of a wife that I am travelling in England."

He paused, and gazed proudly on the scenery, with the air of a Selkirk. Bevan suppressed the obvious comment on the surprising termination of the Frenchman's narrative. He only remarked, "Then you were not guillotined?"

"I was not, sir," retorted the other passionately. "At that time capital punishment was never inflicted in France, though not officially abrogated. I may say," he added, with the pride of a legislator, "that my action lent considerable strength to the agitation which led to its reintroduction.

"No, sir, I was not guillotined. I was sentenced to perpetual imprisonment in Devil's Island." He shuddered. "Can you imagine that accursed Isle? Can your fancy paint one tithe of its horror? Can nightmare itself shadow that inferno, that limbo of the damned? My language is strong, sir; but no language can depict that hell. I will spare you the description. Sand, vermin, crocodiles, venomous snakes, miasma, mosquitoes, fever, filth, toil, jaundice, malaria, starvation, foul undergrowth, weedy swamps breathing out death, hideous and bloated trees of poison, themselves already poisoned by their earth, heat unendurable, insufferable, intolerable, unbearable (as the *Daily Telegraph* said at the time of the Dreyfus case), heat continuous and stifling, no breeze but the pestilential stench of the lagoon, heat that turned the skin into a raging sea of irritation to which the very stings of the mosquitoes and centipedes came as a relief, the interminable task of the day beneath the broiling sun, the lash on every slightest infraction of the harsh prison rules, or even of the laws of politeness toward our warders, men only one degree less damned than we ourselves—all this was nothing. The only amusement of the governors of such a place is cruelty; and their own discomfort makes them more ingenious than all the inquisitors of Spain, than Arabs in their religious frenzy, than Burmans and Kachens and Shans in their Buddhist hatred of all living men, than even the Chinese in their cold lust of cruelty. The governor was a profound psychologist; no corner of the mind that he did not fathom, so as to devise a means of twisting it to torture.

"I remember one of us who took pleasure in keeping his spade bright—it was the regulation that spades must be kept bright, a torture in itself in such a place, where mildew grows on everything as fast almost as snow falls in happier climates. Well, sir, the governor found out that this man took a pleasure in the glint of the sun on the steel, and he forbade that man to clean his spade. A trifle, indeed. What do you know of what prisoners think of trifles? The man went raving mad, and for no other reason. It seemed to him that such detailed refinement of cruelty was a final proof of the innate and inherent devilishness of the universe. Insanity is the logical consequence of such a faith. No, sir, I will spare you the description."

Bevan thought that there had already been too much description, and in his complacent English way surmised that Duguesclin was exaggerating, as he was aware that Frenchmen did. But he only remarked that it must have been terrible. He would have given a good deal, now, to have avoided the conversation. It was not altogether nice to be on a lonely platform with a self-confessed multiple murderer, who had presumably escaped only by a further and extended series of crimes.

"But you ask," pursued Duguesclin, "you ask how I escaped? That, sir, is the story I propose to tell you. My previous remarks have been but preliminary; they have no pertinence or interest, I am aware; but they were necessary, since you so kindly expressed interest in my personality, my family history—heroic (I may claim it) as is the one, and tragic (no one will deny it) as is the other."

Bevan again reflected that his interlocutor must be as bad a psychologist as the governor of Devil's Island was a good one; for he had neither expressed nor felt the slightest concern with either of these matters.

"Well, sir, to my story! Among the convicts there was one universal pleasure, a pleasure that could cease only with life or with the empire of the reason, a pleasure that the governor might (and did) indeed restrict, but could not take away. I refer to hope—the hope of escape. Yes, sir, that spark (alone of all its ancient fires) burnt in this breast—and in that of my fellow-convicts. And in this I did not look so much to myself as to another. I am not endowed with any great intellect," he modestly pursued, "my grandmother was pure English, a Higginbotham, one of the Warwickshire Higginbothams" (what has that to do with his stupidity? thought Bevan) "and the majority of my companions were men not only devoid of intelligence, but of education. The one pinnacled exception was the great Dodu—ha! *you* start?" Bevan had not done anything of the sort; he had continued to exhibit the most stolid indifference to the story.

"Yes, you are not mistaken; it was indeed the world-famous philosopher, the discoverer of Dodium, rarest of known elements, supposed only to exist in the universe to the extent of the thirty-thousand and fifth part of a milligramme, and that in the star called Pegasi; it was Dodu who has shattered the logical process of obversion, and reduced the quadrangle of oppositions to the condition of the British square at Abu-Klea. So much you know; but this perhaps you did not know, that, although a civilian, he was the greatest strategist of France. It was he who in his cabinet made the dispositions of the armies of the Ardennes; and the 1890 scheme of the fortifications of Luneville was due to his genius alone. For this reason the Government were loth to condemn him, though public opinion revolted bitterly against his crime. You remember that, having proved that women after the age of fifty were a useless burden to the State, he had demonstrated his belief by decapitating and devouring his widowed mother. It was consequently the intention of the Government to connive at his escape on the voyage, and to continue to employ him under an assumed name in a flat in an entirely different quarter of Paris. However, the Government fell suddenly; a rival ousted him, and his sentence was carried out with as much severity as if he had been a common criminal.

"It was to such a man (naturally) that I looked to devise a plan for our escape. But rack my brains as I would—my grandmother was a Warwickshire Higginbotham —I could devise no means of getting into touch with him. He must, however, have divined my wishes; for, one day after he had been about a month upon the island (I had been there seven months myself) he stumbled and fell as if struck by the sun at a moment when I was close to him. And as he lay upon the ground he managed to pinch my ankle three times. I caught his glance—he hinted rather than gave me the sign of recognition of the fraternity of Freemasons. Are you a Mason?"

"I am Past Provincial Deputy Grand Sword-Bearer of this province," returned Bevan. "I founded Lodge 14,883, 'Boetic' and Lodge 17,212, 'Colenso'. And I am Past Grand Haggai in my Provincial Grand Chapter."

"I knew it!" exclaimed Duguesclin enthusiastically.

Bevan began to dislike this conversation exceedingly. Did this man—this criminal—know who he was? He knew he was a J.P., that his mother was alive, and now his Masonic dignities. He distrusted this Frenchman more and more. Was the story but a pretext for the demand of a loan? The stranger looked prosperous and had a first class ticket. More likely a black-mailer; perhaps he knew of other things—say that affair at Oxford—or the incident of the Edgware Road—or the matter of Esme Holland. He determined to be more than ever on his guard.

"You will understand with what joy," continued Duguesclin, innocent or careless of the sinister thoughts which occupied his companion, "I received and answered this unmistakable token of friendship. That day no further opportunity of intercourse occurred, but I narrowly watched him on the morrow, and saw that he was dragging his feet in an irregular way. Ha! thought I, a drag for long, an ordinary pace for short. I imitated him eagerly, giving the Morse letter A. His alert mind grasped instantly my meaning; he altered his code (which had been of a different order) and replied with a Morse B on my own system. I answered C; he returned D.

From that moment we could talk fluently and freely as if we were on the terrace of the Cafe de la Paix in our beloved Paris. However, conversation in such circumstances is a lengthy affair. During the whole march to our work he only managed to say, 'Escape soon—please God.' Before his crime he had been an atheist. I was indeed glad to find that punishment had brought repentance."

Bevan himself was relieved. He had carefully refrained from admitting the existence of a French Freemason; that one should have repented filled him with a sense of almost personal triumph. He began to like Duguesclin, and to believe in him. His wrong had been hideous; if his vengeance seemed excessive and even indiscriminate, was not he a Frenchman? Frenchmen do these things! And after all Frenchmen were men. Bevan felt a great glow of benevolence; he remembered that he was not only a man, but a Christian. He determined to set the stranger at his ease.

"Your story interests me intensely," said he. "I sympathise *deeply* with you in your wrongs and in your sufferings. I am heartily thankful that you have escaped, and I beg of you to proceed with the narration of your adventures."

Duguesclin needed no such encouragement. His attitude, from that of the listless weariness with which he had descended from the train, had become animated, sparkling, fiery; he was carried away by the excitement of his passionate memories.

"On the second day Dodu was able to explain his mind. 'If we escape, it must be by a stratagem,' he signalled. It was an obvious remark; but Dodu had no reason to think highly of my intelligence. 'By a stratagem,' he repeated with emphasis.

" 'I have a plan,' he continued. 'It will take twenty- three days to communicate, if we are not interrupted; between three and four months to prepare; two hours and eight minutes to execute. It is theoretically possible to escape by air, by water, or by earth. But as we are watched day and night, it would be useless to try to drive a tunnel to the mainland; we have no aeroplanes or balloons, or means of making them. But if we could once reach the water's edge, which we must do in whatever direction we set out if we only keep in a straight line, and if we can find a boat unguarded, and if we can avoid arousing the alarm, then we have merely to cross the sea, and either find a land where we are unknown, or disguise ourselves and our boat and return to Devil's Island as shipwrecked mariners. The latter idea would be foolish. You will say that the Governor would know that Dodu would not be such a fool; but more, he would know also that Dodu would not be such a fool as to try to take advantage of that circumstance; and he would be right, curse him!'

"It implies the intensest depth of feeling to curse in the Morse code with one's feet—ah! how we hated him.

"Dodu explained to me that he was telling me these obvious things for several reasons: (1) to gauge my intelligence by my reception of them; (2) to make sure that if we failed it should be by my stupidity and not by his neglect to inform me of every detail; (3) because he had acquired the professorial habit as another man might have the gout.

"Briefly, however, this was his plan; to elude the guards, make for the coast, capture a boat, and put to sea. Do you understand? Do you get the idea?"

Bevan replied that it seemed to him the only possible plan.

"A man like Dodu," pursued Duguesclin, "takes nothing for granted. He leaves no precaution untaken; in his plans, if chance be an element, it is an element whose value is calculated to twenty-eight places of decimals.

"But hardly had he laid down these bold outlines of his scheme when interruption came. On the fourth day of our intercourse he signalled only 'Wait. Watch me!' again and again.

"In the evening he manoeuvred to get to the rear of the line of convicts, and only then dragged out 'There is a traitor, a spy. Henceforth I must find a new means of communicating the details of my plan. I have thought it all out. I shall speak in a sort of rebus, which not even you will be able to understand unless you have all the pieces—and the key. Mind you engrave upon your memory every word I say.'

"The following day: 'Do you remember the taking of the old mill by the Prussians in '70? My difficulty is that I must give you the skeleton of the puzzle, which I can't do in words. But watch the line of my spade and my heelmarks, and take a copy.'

"I did this with the utmost minuteness of accuracy and obtained this figure. At my autopsy," said Duguesclin, dramatically, "this should be found engraved upon my heart."

He drew a notebook from his pocket, and rapidly sketched the subjoined figure for the now interested Bevan.

"You will note that the figure has eight sides, and that twenty-seven crosses are disposed in groups of three, while in one corner is a much larger and thicker cross and two smaller crosses not so symmetrical. This group represents the element of chance; and you will at least gain a hint of the truth if you reflect that eight is the cube of two, and twenty-seven of three."

Bevan looked intelligent.

"On the return march," continued Duguesclin, "Dodu said, 'The spy is on the watch. But count the letters in the name of Aristotle's favourite disciple.' I guessed (as he intended me to do) that he did not mean Aristotle. He wished to suggest Plato, and so Socrates; hence I counted A-L-C-I-B-I-A-D-E-S = 10, and thus completely baffled the spy for that day. The following day he rapped out 'Rahu' very emphatically, meaning that the next lunar eclipse would be the proper moment for our evasion, and spent the rest of the day in small talk, so as to lull the suspicions of the spy. For three days he had no opportunity of saying anything, being in the hospital with fever. On the fourth day: 'I have discovered that spy is a damned swine of an opium- smoking lieutenant from Toulon. We have him; he doesn't know Paris. Now then—draw a line from the Gare de l'Est to the Etoile; erect an equilateral triangle on that line. Think of the name of the world-famous man who lives at the apex.' (This was a touch of super-genius, as it forced me to use the English alphabet for the basis of the cipher, and the spy spoke no language but his own, except a little Swiss.) 'From this time I shall communicate in a cipher of the direct additive numerical order, and the key shall be his name.'

"It was only my incomparably strong constitution which enabled me to add the task of deciphering his conversation to that imposed by Government. To memorise perfectly a cipher communication of half-an-hour is no mean feat of mnemonics, especially when the deciphered message is itself couched in the obscurest symbolism. The spy must have thought his reason in danger if he succeeded in reading the hieroglyphs which were the mere pieces of the puzzle of the master-thinker. For instance, I would get a message; which, when deciphered (and the spy would gnash his teeth every time Dodu signalled a W), only meant: 'The peaches of 1761 are luminous in the gardens of Versailles.'

"Or again: 'Hunt; the imprisoned Pope; the Pompadour; the Stag and Cross. 'The men of the fourth of September; their leader divided by the letters of the Victim of the Eighth of Thermidor.' 'Crillon was unfortunate that day, though braver than ever.'

"Such were the indications from which I sought to piece together our plan of escape!

"Perhaps rather by intuition than by reason, I gathered from some two hundred of such clues that the guards Bertrand, Rolland, and Monet, had been bribed, and also promised advancement, and (above all) removal from the hated Island, should they connive at our escape. It seemed that the Government had still use for its first strategist. The eclipse was due some ten weeks ahead, and needed neither bribe nor promise. The difficulty was to ensure the presence of Bertrand as sentinel in our corridor, Rolland at the ring-fence, and Monet at the outposts. The chances against such a combination at the eclipse were infinitesimal.

"It would have been madness to trust to luck in so essential a matter. Dodu set to work to bribe the Governor himself. This was unfortunately impossible; for (a) no one could approach the governor even by means of the intermediary of the bribed guards; (b) the offence for which he had been promoted to the governorship was of a nature unpardonable by any Government. He was in reality more a prisoner than ourselves; (c) he was a man of immense wealth, assured career, and known probity.

"I cannot now enter into his history, which you no doubt know in any case. I will only say that it was of such a character that these facts (of so curiously contradictory appearance—on the face of it) apply absolutely. However the tone of confidence which thrilled in Dodu's messages, 'Pluck grapes in Burgundy; press vats in Cognac; ha!' 'The souffle with the nuts in it is ready for us by the Seine,' and the like, showed me that his giant brain had not only grappled with the problem, but solved it to his satisfaction. The plan was perfect; on the night of the eclipse those three guards would be on duty at such and such gates; Dodu would tear his clothes into strips, bind and gag Bertrand, come and release me. Together we should spring on Rolland, take his uniform and rifle, and leave him bound and gagged. We should then dash for the shore, do the same with Monet, and then, dressed in their uniforms, take the boat of an octopus-fisher, row to the harbour, and ask in the name of the governor for the use of his steam yacht to chase an escaped fugitive. We should then steam into the track of ships and set fire to the yacht, so as to be 'rescued' and conveyed to England, whence we could arrange with the French Government for rehabilitation.

"Such was the simple yet subtle plan of Dodu. Down to the last detail was it perfected—until one fatal day.

"The spy, stricken by yellow fever, dropped suddenly dead in the fields before noon 'Cease work' had sounded. Instantly, without a moment's hesitation, Dodu strode across to me and said, at the risk of the lash: 'The whole plan which I have explained to you in cipher these last four months is a blind. That spy knew all. His lips are sealed in death. I have another plan, the real plan, simpler and surer. I will tell it to you tomorrow.'

The whistle of an approaching engine interrupted this tragic episode of the adventures of Duguesclin.

" 'Yes,' said Dodu" (continued the narrator), " 'I have a better plan. I have a stratagem. I will tell it you tomorrow.'

The train which was to carry the narrator and his hearer to Mudchester came round the corner. "That morrow," glowered Duguesclin, "that morrow never came. The same sun that slew the spy broke the great brain of Dodu; that very afternoon, a gibbering maniac, they thrust him in the padded room, never again to emerge."

The train drew up at the platform of the little junction. He almost hissed in Bevan's face.

"It was not Dodu at all," he screamed, "it was a common criminal, an epileptic; he should never have been sent to Devil's Island at all. He had been mad for months. His messages had no sense at all; it was a cruel practical joke!"

"But how," said Bevan getting into his carriage and looking back, "how did you escape in the end?"

"By a stratagem," replied the Irishman, and jumped into another compartment.

The Magick Cup

As the Magick Wand is the Will, the Wisdom, the Word of the Magician, so is the Magick Cup his Understanding.

This is the cup of which it was written: "Father, if it by Thy Will, let this cup pass from Me!" And again: "Can ye drink of the cup that I drink of?"

And it is also the cup in the hand of OUR LADY BABALON, and the cup of the Sacrament.

This Cup is full of bitterness, and of blood, and of intoxication.

The Understanding of the Magus is his link with the Invisible, on the passive side.

His Will errs actively by opposing itself to the Universal Will.

His Understanding errs passively when it receives influence from that which is not the ultimate truth.

In the beginning the Cup of the student is almost empty; and even such truth as he receives may leak away, and be lost.

They say that the Venetians made glasses which changed colour if poison was put into them; of such a glass must the student make his Cup.

Very little experience on the mystic path will show him that of all the impressions he receives none is true. Either they are false in themselves, or they are wrongly interpreted in his mind.

There is one truth, and only one. All other thoughts are false.

And as he advances in the knowledge of his mind he will come to understand that its whole structure is so faulty that it is quite incapable, even in its most exalted moods, of truth.

He will recognize that any thought merely establishes a relation between the Ego and the non-Ego.

Kant has shown that even the laws of nature are but the conditions of thought. And as the current of thought is the blood of the mind, it is said that the Magick Cup is filled with the blood of the Saints. **All thought must be offered up as a sacrifice.**

The Cup can hardly be described a weapon. It is round like the pantacle--not straight like the wand and the dagger, Reception, not projection, is its nature.

So that which is round to him is a symbol of the influence from the higher. This circle symbolizes the Infinite, as every cross or Tau represents the Finite. That which is four square shows the Finite fixed into itself; for this reason the altar is foursquare. It is the solid basis from which all the operation proceeds. One form of magical cup has a sphere beneath the bowl, and is supported on a conical base.

This cup (crescent, sphere, cone) represents the three principals of the Moon, the Sun, and Fire, the three principles which, according to the Hindus, have course in the body.

This is the cup of purification; as Zoroaster says:

"So therefore first the priest who governeth the works of fire must sprinkle with the lustral water of the loud-resounding sea."

It is the sea that purifies the world. And the "Great Sea" is in the Qabalah a name of Binah, "Understanding."

It is by the Understanding of the Magus that his work is purified.

Binah, moreover, is the Moon, and the bowl of this cup is shaped like the moon.

This moon is the path of Gimel through which the influence from the Crown descends upon the Sun of Tiphereth.

And this is based upon the pyramid of fire which symbolizes the aspiration of the student.

In Hindu symbolism the Amrita or "dew of immortality" drips constantly upon a man, but is burnt up by the gross fire of his appetites. Yogis attempt to catch and so preserve this dew by turning back the tongue in the mouth.

Concerning the water in this Cup, it may be said that just as the wand should be perfectly rigid, the ideal solid, so should the water be the ideal fluid.

The Wand is erect, and must extend to Infinity.

The surface of the water is flat, and must extend to Infinity.

One is the line, the other the plane.

But as the Wand is weak without breadth, so is the water false without depth. The Understanding of the Magus must include all things, and that understanding must be infinitely profound.

H. G. Wells has said that "every word of which a man is ignorant represents an idea of which he is ignorant." And it is impossible perfectly to understand all things unless all things be first known.

Understanding is the structuralization of knowledge.

All impressions are disconnected, as the Babe of the Abyss is so terribly aware; and the Master of the Temple must sit for 106 seasons in the City of Pyramids because this coordination is a tremendous task.

There is nothing particularly occult in this doctrine concerning knowledge and understanding.

A looking-glass receives all impressions and coordinates none.

The savage has none but the most simple associations of ideas.

Even the ordinary civilized man goes very little further.

All advance in thought is made by collecting the greatest possible number of facts, classifying them, and grouping them.

The philologist, though perhaps he only speaks one language, has a much higher type of mind than the linguist who speaks twenty.

This Tree of Thought is exactly paralleled by the tree of nervous structure.

Very many people go about nowadays who are exceedingly "well-informed," but who have not the slightest idea of the meaning of the facts they know. They have not developed that necessary higher part of the brain. Induction is impossible to them.

This capacity for storing away facts is compatible with actual imbecility. Some imbeciles have been able to store their memories with more knowledge than perhaps any sane man could hope to acquire.

This is the great fault of modern education--a child is stuffed with facts, and no attempt is made to explain their connection and bearing. The result is that even the facts themselves are soon forgotten.

Any first-rate mind is insulted and irritated by such treatment, and any first-rate memory is in danger of being spoilt by it.

No two ideas have any real meaning until they are harmonized in a third, and the operation is only perfect when these ideas are contradictory. This is the essence of the Hegelian logic.

The Magick Cup, as was shown above, is also the flower. It is the lotus which opens to the sun, and which collects the dew.

This Lotus is in the hand of Isis the great Mother. It is a symbol similar to the Cup in the hand of OUR LADY BABALON.

There are also the Lotuses in the human body, according to the Hindu system of Physiology.

There is the lotus of three petals in the Sacrum, in which the Kundalini lies asleep. This lotus is the receptacle of reproductive force.

There is also the six-petalled lotus opposite the navel-- which receives the forces which nourish the body.

There is also a lotus in the Solar plexus which receives the nervous forces.

The six-petalled lotus in the heart corresponds to Tiphereth, and receives those vital forces which are connected with the blood.

The sixteen-petalled lotus opposite the larynx receives the nourishment needed by the breath.

The two-petalled lotus of the pineal gland receives the nourishment needed by thought, while above the junction of the cranial sutures is that sublime lotus, of a thousand and one petals, which receives the influence from on high; and in which, in the Adept, the awakened Kundalini takes her pleasure with the Lord of All.

All these lotuses are figured by the Magick Cup.

In man they are but partly opened, or only opened to their natural nourishment. In fact it is better to think of them as closed, as secreting that nourishment, which, because of the lack of sun, turns to poison.

The Magick Cup must have no lid, yet it must be kept veiled most carefully at all times, except when invocation of the Highest is being made.

This Cup must also be hidden from the profane. The Wand must be kept secret lest the profane, fearing it, should succeed in breaking it; the cup lest, wishing to touch it, they should defile it.

Yet the sprinkling of its water not only purifies the Temple, but blesseth them that are without: freely must it be poured! But let no one know your real purpose, and let no one know the secret of your strength. Remember Samson! Remember Guy Fawkes!

Of the methods of increasing Understanding those of the Holy Qabalah are perhaps the best, provided that the intellect is thoroughly awake to their absurdity, and never allows itself to be convinced.

Further meditation of certain sorts is useful: not the strict meditation which endeavours to still the mind, but such a meditation as Sammasati.

On the exoteric side if necessary the mind should be trained by the study of any well-developed science, such as chemistry, or mathematics.

The idea of organization is the first step, that of interpretation the second. The Master of the Temple, whose grade corresponds to Binah, is sworn to interpret every phenomenon as a particular dealing of God with his soul.

But even the beginner may attempt this practice with advantage.

Either a fact fits in or it does not; if it does not, harmony is broken; and as the Universal harmony cannot be broken, the discord must be in the mind of the student, thus showing that he is not in tune with that Universal choir.

Let him then puzzle out first the great facts, then the little; until one summer, when he is bald and lethargic after lunch, he understands and appreciates the existence of flies!

This lack of Understanding with which we all begin is so terrible, so pitiful. In this world there is so much cruelty, so much waste, so much stupidity.

The contemplation of the Universe must be at first almost pure anguish. It is this fact which is responsible for most the speculations of philosophy.

Mediaeval philosophers went hopelessly astray because their theology necessitated the reference of all things to the standard of men's welfare.

They even became stupid: Bernardin de St. Pierre (was it not?) said that the goodness of God was such that wherever men had built a great city, He had placed a river to assist them in conveying merchandise. But the truth is that in no way can we imagine the Universe as devised. If horses were made for men to ride, were not men made for worms to eat?

And so we find once more that **the Ego-idea must be ruthlessy rooted out before Understanding can be attained.**

There is an apparent contradiction between this attitude and that of the Master of the Temple. What can possible be more selfish than this interpretation of everything as the dealing of God with the soul?

But it is God who is all and not any part; and every "dealing" must thus be an expansion of the soul, a destruction of its separateness.

Every ray of the sun expands the flower.

The surface of the water in the Magick Cup is infinite; there is no point different from any other point.

Thus, ultimately, as the wand is a binding and a limitation, so is the Cup an expansion--into the Infinite.

And this is the danger of the Cup; it must necessarily be open to all, and yet if anything is put into it which is out of proportion, unbalanced, or impure, it takes hurt.

And here again we find difficulty with out thoughts. The grossness and stupidity of *simple impressions* cloud the water; *emotions* trouble it; *perceptions* are still far from the perfect purity of truth; they cause reflections; while the *tendencies* alter the refractive index, and break up the light. Even *consciousness* itself is that which distinguishes between the lower and the higher, the waters which are below the firmament from the waters which are above the firmament, that appalling stage in the great curse of creation.

Since at the best this water is but a reflection, how tremendously important it becomes that it should be still!

If the cup is shaken the light will be broken up.

Therefore the Cup is placed upon the Altar, which is foursquare, will multiplied by will, the confirmation of the will in the Magical Oath, its fixation in Law.

It is easy to see when water is muddy, and easy to get rid of the mud; but there are many impurities which defy everything but distillation and even some which must be fractionated unto 70 times 7.

There is, however, a universal solvent and harmonizer, a certain dew which is so pure that a single drop of it cast into the water of the Cup will for the time being bring all to perfection.

This dew is called Love. Even as in the case of human love, the whole Universe appears perfect to the man who is under its control, so is it, and much more, with the Divine Love of which it is now spoken.

For human love is an excitement, and not a stilling, of the mind; and as it is bound to the individual, only leads to greater trouble in the end.

This Divine Love, on the contrary, is attached to no symbol.

It abhors limitation, either in its intensity or its scope. And this is the dew of the stars of which it is spoken in the Holy Books, for NUIT the Lady of the Stars is called the "continuous one of Heaven," and it is that Dew which bathes the body of the Adept "in a sweet-smelling perfume of sweat."

In this cup, therefore, though all things are placed, by virtue of this dew all lose their identity. And therefore this Cup is in the hand of BABALON, the Lady of the City of Pyramids, wherein no one can be distinguished from any other, wherein no one may sit until he has lost his name.

Of that which is in the Cup it is also said that it is wine. This is the Cup of Intoxication. Intoxication means poisoning, and in particular refers to the poison in which arrows are dipped. Think of the Vision of the Arrow in Liber 418, and look at the passages in the Holy Books which speak of the action of the spirit under the figure of a deadly poison.

For to each individual thing attainment means first and foremost the destruction of the individuality.

Each of our ideas must be made to give up the Self to the Beloved, so that we may eventually give up the Self to the Beloved in our turn.

It will be remembered in the History Lection how the Adepts "who had with smiling faces abandoned their homes, their possessions…could with steady calm and firm correctness abandon the Great Work itself; for this is the last and greatest projection of the alchemist."

The Master of the Temple has crossed the Abyss, has entered the Palace of the King's Daughter; he has only to utter one word, and all is dissolved. But, instead of that, he is found hidden in the earth, tending a garden.

This mystery is all too complex to be elucidated in these fragments of impure thought; it is a suitable subject for meditation.

Liber Resh vel Helios

These are the adorations to be performed by all aspirants to the A. A.

Let him greet the Sun at dawn, facing East, giving the sign of his grade. And let him say in a loud voice:

Hail unto Thee who art Ra in Thy rising, even unto Thee who art Ra in Thy strength, who travellest over the Heavens in Thy bark at the Uprising of the Sun.
Tahuti standeth in His splendour at the prow, and Ra-Hoor abideth at the helm.
Hail unto Thee from the Abodes of Night!

Also at Noon, let him greet the Sun, facing South, giving the sign of his grade. And let him say in a loud voice:

Hail unto Thee who art Ahathoor in Thy triumphing, even unto Thee who art Ahathoor in Thy beauty, who travellest over the Heavens in Thy bark at the Mid-course of the Sun.
Tahuti standeth in His splendour at the prow, and Ra-Hoor abideth at the helm.
Hail unto Thee from the Abodes of Morning!

Also, at Sunset, let him greet the Sun, facing West, giving the sign of his grade. And let him say in a loud voice:

> *Hail unto Thee who art Tum in Thy setting, even unto Thee who art Tum in Thy joy, who travellest over the Heavens in Thy bark at the Down-going of the Sun.*
>
> *Tahuti standeth in His splendour at the prow, and Ra-Hoor abideth at the helm.*
>
> *Hail unto Thee from the Abodes of Day!*

Lastly, at Midnight, let him greet the Sun, facing North, giving the sign of his grade. And let him say in a loud voice:

> *Hail unto thee who art Khephra in Thy hiding, even unto Thee who art Khephra in Thy silence, who travellest over the Heavens in Thy bark at the Midnight Hour of the Sun.*
>
> *Tahuti standeth in His splendour at the prow, and Ra-Hoor abideth at the helm.*
>
> *Hail unto Thee from the Abodes of Evening.*

And after each of these invocations thou shalt give the sign of silence, and afterwards thou shalt perform the adoration that is taught thee by thy Superior. And then do thou compose Thyself to holy meditation.

Also it is better if in these adorations thou assume the God-form of Whom thou adorest, as if thou didst unite with Him in the adoration of That which is beyond Him.

Thus shalt thou ever be mindful of the Great Work which thou hast undertaken to perform, and thus shalt thou be strengthened to pursue it unto the attainment of the Stone of the Wise, the Summum Bonum, True Wisdom and Perfect Happiness.

The Sabbath

To A. E. W.

Occult, forbidden lights
Move in the royal rites.
Diaphanous, they dance
Above the souls in trance
That have attained to their untold inheritance.

Above the mystic masque,
Like plumes upon a casque,
They wave their purple and red
Above each haggard head.
Thy are like gems snake-rooted, basilisks' bed.

Here were the tables set
For Baal and Baphomet:
Here was the altar drest
With fire and Alkahest
For many a holy host, for many a goodly guest.

Here was the veil, and here
The sword and dagger of fear.
Here was the circle traced,
And here the pillar placed
For Him the utterly unfathomably chaste.

Here grew the murmur grim
Of the low-muttered hymn;
Here sound itself caught flame

From the dark drone of shame—
The world reverberated the unutterable Name!

Astarte from her trance
Leapt loving to the dance,
Greeting as fire greets firs
Her whirling worshippers.
And all her joy was theirs, and all their madness hers!

Yea! thou and I that strove
For mastery in love,
Circling the altar stone
Maze-like, with magic moan,
Forthwith made that divinest destiny our own.

Throughout that violent vigil
We wove the stormy sigil,
Our faces ashen-lipped
From our heart's blood that dripped
On the armed talismans of that moon-vaulted crypt.

Then came the sombre spectre
From the abyss of nectar;
Yea, from the icy North
Came the great vision forth,
A giant breaking through the weary web of wrath.

Then, in the midst, behold
That blaze of burnished gold
Imperishable, set
With adamant and jet;

And by the obscene head we hailed him Baphomet.

Hail to the Master, hail!
Lord of the Sabbath! Baal!
I kiss thy feet, I kiss
Thy knees—and this—and this—
Till I am lifted up to the incorporeal Byss.

Till here alone exalted
I gaze beneath the vaulted
Forehead, within the eyes
Wherein such wonder lies,
The incommensurable gain, the pagan prize.

We are thy moons and suns,
Thy loyal knights and nuns,
Who tread the dance around
Thine altar, with the sound
Of death-sobs echoing through the immemorial ground.

O glee! the price to pay!
Swear but our souls away!
And we may gain the goal
That all the wise extol—
The world, the flesh, the devil, weighed against a soul.

The wind blows from the south!
Crushed to that burning mouth,

Lured by that lurid law,
We melt within that maw;
And all the fiends loose hold, and all the gods withdraw!

Upon the altar-stone
We are alone—alone!
In vivid blackness curled
With livid lightings pearled—
Sweat-drops upon God's brow when He creates a world!

Sister, the word is spoken!
Sister, the spell is broken.
The Sabbath torches flicker;
The Sabbath heart beats quicker;
We have drained the Sabbath cup of its austerest liquor.

Forsaken is the hall;
Finished the festival.
My witch and I are thrown
Dead on the altar stone
By the contemptuous god that made our soul his own.

Come! Come! we must begone.
Hiss the last orison!
Intone the last lament!
Take the last sacrament,
The extreme unction, Saviour when the soul is spent!

Come! hurry through the night,
A trail of tortured flight!
Eagle and pelican
Become mere maid and man
Till the next Sabbath—days each like leviathan!

Nay! lift the languid head!
Take of this wine and bread!
The vision is withdrawn;
The lake calls, and the lawn;
Our love shall walk abroad in the grey hours of dawn!

The Cry of the 12th Aethyr, which is Called LOE

There appear in the stone two pillars of flame, and in the midst is a chariot of white fire.

This seems to be the chariot of the Seventh Key of Tarot. But it is drawn by four sphinxes, diverse, like the four sphinxes upon the door of the vault of the adepts, counterchanged in their component parts.

The chariot itself is the lunar crescent, waning. The canopy is supported by eight pillars of amber. These pillars are upright, and yet the canopy which they support is the whole vault of the night.

The charioteer is a man in golden armour, studded with sapphires, but over his shoulders is a white robe, and over that a red robe. Upon his golden helmet he beareth for his crest a crab. His hands are clasped upon a cup, from which radiates a ruddy glow, constantly increasing, so that everything is blotted out by its glory, and the whole Aire is filled with it.

And there is a marvelous perfume in the Aire, like unto the perfume of Ra Hoor Khuit, but sublimated, as if the quintessence of that perfume alone were burnt. For it hath the richness and voluptuousness and humanity of blood, and the strength and freshness of meal, and the sweetness of honey, and the purity of olive-oil, and the holiness of that oil which is made of myrrh, and cinnamon, and galangal.

The charioteer speaks in a low, solemn voice, awe inspiring, like a large and very distant bell: Let him look upon the cup whose blood is mingled therein, for the wine of the cup is the blood of the saints. Glory unto the Scarlet Woman, Babalon the Mother of Abominations, that rideth upon the Beast, for she hath spilt their blood in every corner of the earth and lo! she hath mingled it in the cup of her whoredom.

With the breath of her kisses hath she fermented it, and it hath become the wine of the Sacrament, the wine of the Sabbath; and in the Holy Assembly hath she poured it out for her worshippers, and they had become drunken thereon, so that face to face they beheld my Father. Thus are they made worthy to become partakers of the Mystery of this holy vessel, for the blood is the life. So sitteth she from age to age, and the righteous are never weary of her kisses, and by her murders and fornications she seduceth the world. Therein is manifested the glory of my Father, who is truth.

(This wine is such that its virtue radiateth through the cup, and I reel under the intoxication of it. And every thought is destroyed by it. It abideth alone, and its name is Compassion. I understand by "Compassion," the sacrament of suffering, partaken by the true worshippers of the Highest. And it is an ecstasy in which there is no trace of pain. Its passivity (=passion) is like the giving-up of the self to the beloved.)

The voice continues: This is the Mystery of Babylon, the Mother of abominations, and this is the mystery of her adulteries, for she hath yielded up herself to everything that liveth, and hath become a partaker in its mystery. And because she hath made herself the servant of each, therefore is she become the mistress of all. Not as yet canst thou comprehend her glory.

Beautiful art thou, O Babylon, and desirable, for thou hast given thyself to everything that liveth, and thy weakness hath subdued their strength. For in that union thou didst *understand*. Therefore art thou called Understanding, O Babylon, Lady of the Night!

This is that which is written, "O my God, in one last rapture let me attain to the union with the many." For she is Love, and her love is one, and she hath divided the one love into infinite loves, and each love is one, and equal to The One, and therefore is she passed "from the assembly and the law and the enlightenment unto the anarchy of solitude and darkness. For ever thus must she veil the brilliance of Her Self."

O Babylon, Babylon, thou mighty Mother, that ridest upon the crowned beast, let me be drunken upon the wine of thy fornications; let thy kisses wanton me unto death, that even I, thy cup-bearer, may *understand*.

Now, through the ruddy glow of the cup, I may perceive far above, and infinitely great, the vision of Babylon. And the Beast whereon she rideth is the Lord of the City of the Pyramids, that I beheld in the fourteenth Ethyr. Now that is gone in the glow of the cup, and the Angel saith: Not as yet mayest thou understand the mystery of the Beast, for it pertaineth not unto the mystery of this Aire, and few that are new-born unto Understanding are capable thereof.

The cup glows ever brighter and fierier. All my sense is unsteady, being smitten with ecstasy.

And the Angel sayeth: Blessed are the saints, that their blood is mingled in the cup, and can never be separate any more. For Babylon the Beautiful, the Mother of abominations, hath sworn by her holy cteis, whereof every point is a pang, that she will not rest from her adulteries until the blood of everything that liveth is gathered therein, and the wine thereof laid up and matured and consecrated, and worthy to gladden the heart of my Father. For my Father is weary with the stress of eld, and cometh not to her bed. Yet shall this perfect wine be the quintessence, and the elixir, and by the draught thereof shall he renew his youth; and so shall it be eternally, as age by age the worlds do dissolve and change, and the universe unfoldeth itself as a Rose, and shutteth itself up as the Cross that is bent into the cube.

And this is the comedy of Pan, that is played at night in the thick forest. And this is the mystery of Dionysus Zagreus, that is celebrated upon the holy mountain of Kithairon. And this is the secret of the brothers of the Rosy Cross; and this is the heart of the ritual that is accomplished in the Vault of the Adepts that is hidden in the Mountain of the Caverns, even the Holy Mountain Abiegnus.

And this is the meaning of the Supper of the Passover, the spilling of the blood of the Lamb being a ritual of the Dark Brothers, for they have sealed up the Pylon with blood, lest the Angel of Death should enter therein. Thus do they shut themselves off from the company of the saints. Thus do they keep themselves from compassion and from understanding. Accursed are they, for they shut up their blood in their heart.

They keep themselves from the kisses of my Mother Babylon, and in their lonely fortresses they pray to the false moon. And they bind themselves together with an oath, and with a great curse. And of their malice they conspire together, and they have power, and mastery, and in their cauldrons do they brew the harsh wine of delusion, mingled with the poison of their selfishness.

Thus they make war upon the Holy One, sending forth their delusion upon men, and upon everything that liveth. So that their false compassion is called compassion, and their false understanding is called understanding, for this is their most potent spell.

Yet of their own poison do they perish, and in their lonely fortresses shall they be eaten up by Time that hath cheated them to serve him, and by the mighty devil Choronzon, their master, whose name is the Second Death, for the blood that they have sprinkled on their Pylon, that is a bar against the Angel Death, is the key by which he entereth in.

The Angel sayeth: And this is the word of double power in the voice of the Master, wherein the Five interpenetrateth the Six. This is its secret interpretation that may not be understood, save only of *them that understand*. And for this is the Key of the Pylon of Power, because there is no power that may endure, save only the power that descendeth in this my chariot from Babylon, the city of the Fifty Gates, the Gate of the God *On*. Moreover is *On* the Key of the Vault that is 120. So also do the Majesty and the Beauty derive from the Supernal Wisdom.

But this is a mystery utterly beyond thine understanding. For Wisdom is the Man, and Understanding the Woman, and not until thou hast perfectly understood canst thou begin to be wise. But I reveal unto thee a mystery of the Ethyrs, that not only are they bound up with the Sephiroth, but also with the Paths. Now, the plane of the Ethyrs interpenetrateth and surroundeth the universe wherein the Sephiroth are established, and therefore is the order of the Ethyrs not the order of the Tree of Life. And only in a few places do they coincide. But the knowledge of the Ethyrs is deeper than the knowledge of the Sephiroth, for that in the Ethyrs is the knowledge of the Eons, and of Thelema. And to each shall it be given according to his capacity. (He has been saying certain secret things to the unconscious mind of the seer, of a personal nature.)

Now a voice comes from without: And lo! I saw you to the end.

And a great bell begins to toll. And there come six little children out of the floor of the chariot, and in their hands is a veil so fine and transparent that it is hardly visible. Yet, when they put it over the Cup, the Angel bowing his head reverently, the light of the Cup goes out entirely. And as the light of the Cup vanishes, it is like a swift sunset in the whole Aire, for it was from the light of that Cup alone that it was lighted.

And now the light is all gone out of the stone, and I am very cold.

BOU-SAʿADA.
December 4 - 5, 1909. 11.30 p.m.-1.20 a.m.

Absinthe: The Green Goddess
I.

Keep always this dim corner for me, that I may sit while the Green Hour glides, a proud pavane of Time. For I am no longer in the city accursed, where Time is horsed on the white gelding Death, his spurs rusted with blood.

There is a corner of the United States which he has overlooked. It lies in New Orleans, between Canal street and Esplanade avenue; the Mississippi for its base. Thence it reaches northward to a most curious desert land, where is a cemetery lovely beyond dreams, its walls low and whitewashed, within which straggles a wilderness of strange and fantastic tombs; and hard by is that great city of brothels which is so cynically mirthful a neighbor. As Félicien Rops wrote, — or was it Edmond d'Haraucourt? — *la Prostitution et la Mort sont frère et soeur — les fils de Dieu!* At least the poet of La Légende des Sexes was right, and the psycho-analysts after him, in identifying the Mother with the Tomb. This, then, is only the beginning and end of things, this "quartier macabre" beyond the North Rampart; and the Mississippi on the other side, is like the space between, our life which flows, and fertilizes as it flows, muddy and malarious as it may be, to empty itself into the warm bosom of the Gulf Stream, which (in our allegory) we may call the Life of God.

But our business is with the heart of things; we must go beyond the crude phenomena of nature if we are to dwell in the spirit. Art is the soul of life; and the Old Absinthe House is heart and soul of the old quarter of New Orleans.

For here was the headquarters of no common man — no less than a real pirate — of Captain Lafitte, who not only robbed his neighbors, but defended them against invasion. Here, too, sat Henry Clay, who lived and died to give his name to a cigar. Outside this house no man remembers much more of him than that; but here, authentic and, as I imagine, indignant, his ghost stalks grimly.

Here, too, are marble basins hollowed — and hallowed! — by the drippings of the water which creates by baptism the new spirit of absinthe.

I am only sipping the second glass of that "fascinating, but subtle poison, whose ravages eat men's heart and brain" that I have ever tasted in my life; and as I am not an American anxious for quick action, I am not surprised and disappointed that I do not drop dead upon the spot. But I can taste souls without the aid of absinthe; and besides, this is magic absinthe! The spirit of the house has entered into it; it is an elixir, the masterpiece of an old alchemist, no common wine.

And so, as I talk with the patron concerning the vanity of things, I perceive the secret of the heart of God himself; this, that everything, even the vilest thing, is so unutterably lovely that it is worthy of the devotion of a God for all eternity.

What other excuse could He give man for making him? In substance, that is my answer to King Solomon.

II.

The barrier between divine and human things is frail but inviolable; the artist and the bourgeois are only divided by a point of view. "A hair divides the false and true."

I am watching the opalescence of my absinthe, and it leads me to ponder upon a certain very curious mystery, persistent in legend. We may call it the mystery of the rainbow.

Originally, in the fantastic but significant legend of the Hebrews, the rainbow is mentioned as the sign of salvation. The world had been purified by water, and was ready for the revelation of Wine. God would never again destroy his work, but ultimately seal its perfection by a baptism of fire.

Now, in this analogue also falls the coat of many colors which was made for Joseph, a legend which was regarded as so important that it was subsequently borrowed for the romance of Jesus. The veil of the Temple, too, was of many colors. We find, further east, that the Manipura Cakkra — the Lotus of the City of Jewels — which is an important centre in Hindu anatomy, and apparently identical with the solar plexus, is the central point of the nervous system of the human body, dividing the sacred from the profane, or the lower from the higher.

In western Mysticism, once more we learn that the middle grade of initiation is called Hodos Camelionis, the Path of the Cameleon; there is here evidently an allusion to this same mystery. We also learn that the middle stage in Alchemy is when the liquor becomes opalescent.

Finally, we note among the visions of the Saints one called the Universal Peacock, in which the totality of things is perceived thus royally apparelled.

Would it were possible to assemble in this place the cohorts of quotation; for indeed they are beautiful with banners, flashing their myriad rays from cothurn and habergeon, gay and gallant in the light of that Sun which knows no fall from Zenith of high noon!

Yet I must needs already have written so much to make clear one pitiful conceit: can it be that in the opalescence of absinthe is some occult link with this mystery of the Rainbow? For undoubtedly one glass does indefinably and subtly insinuate the drinker within the secret chamber of Beauty, does kindle his thoughts to rapture, adjust his point of view to that of the artist, at least in that degree of which he is originally capable, weave for his fancy a gala dress of stuff as many-coloured as the mind of Aphrodite.

Oh Beauty! Long did I love thee, long did I pursue thee, thee elusive, thee intangible! And lo! thou enfoldest me by night and day in the arms of gracious, of luxurious, of shimmering silence.

III.

The Prohibitionist must always be a person of no moral character; for he cannot even conceive of the possibility of a man capable of resisting temptation. Still more, he is so obsessed, like the savage, by the fear of the unknown, that he regards alcohol as a fetish, necessarily alluring and tyrannical.

With this ignorance of human nature goes an even grosser ignorance of the divine nature.

He does not understand that the universe has only one possible purpose; that, the business of life being happily completed by the production of the necessities and luxuries incidental to comfort, the residuum of human energy needs an outlet. The surplus of Will must find issue in the elevation of the individual towards the godhead; and the method of such elevation is by religion, love, and art. Now these three things are indissolubly bound up with wine, for they are themselves species of intoxication.

Yet against all these things we find the prohibitionist, logically enough. It is true that he usually pretends to admit religion as a proper pursuit for humanity; but what a religion! He has removed from it every element of ecstasy or even of devotion; in his hands it has become cold, fanatical, cruel, and stupid, a thing merciless and formal, without sympathy or humanity. Love and art he rejects altogether; for him the only meaning of love is a mechanical — hardly even physiological! — process necessary for the perpetuation of the human race. (But why perpetuate it?) Art is for him the parasite and pimp of love; he cannot distinguish between the Apollo Belvedere and the crude bestialities of certain Pompeian frescoes, or between Rabelais and Elinor Glyn.

What then is his ideal of human life? One cannot say. So crass a creature can have no true ideal. There have been ascetic philosophers; but the prohibitionist would be as offended by their doctrine as by ours. These, indeed, are not so dissimilar as appears. Wage-slavery and boredom seem to complete his outlook on the world.

There are species which survive because of the feeling of disgust inspired by them; one is reluctant to set the heel firmly upon them, however thick may be one's boots. But when they are recognized as utterly noxious to humanity — the more so that they ape its form — then courage must be found, or, rather, nausea must be swallowed. May God send us a Saint George!

IV.

It is notorious that all genius is accompanied by vice. Almost always this takes the form of sexual extravagance. It is to be observed that deficiency, as in the cases of Carlyle and Ruskin, is to be reckoned as extravagance. At least, the word abnormality will fit all cases. Farther, we see that in a very large number of great men there has also been indulgence in drink or drugs. There are whole periods when practically every great man has been thus marked; these periods are those during which the heroic spirit has died out of their nation, and the bourgeois is apparently triumphant.

In this case the cause is evidently the horror of life induced in the artist by the contemplation of his surroundings. He must find another world, no matter at what cost.

Consider the end of the eighteenth century. In France, at that time, the men of genius were made, so to speak, possible, by the Revolution. In England, under Castlereagh, we find Blake lost to humanity in mysticism, Shelley and Byron exiles, Coleridge taking refuge in opium, Keats sinking under the weight of circumstance, Wordsworth forced to sell his soul, while the enemy, in the persons of Southey and Moore, triumphantly holds sway.

The poetically similar period in France is 1850 to 1870. Hugo is in exile, and all his brethren are given to absinthe or to hashish or to opium.

There is however another consideration more important. There are some men who possess the understanding of the City of God, and know not the keys; or, if they possess them, have not force to turn them in the wards. Such men often seek to win heaven by forged credentials. Just so a youth who desires love is too often deceived by simulacra, embraces Lydia thinking her to be Lalage.

But the greatest men of all suffer neither the limitations of the former class nor the illusions of the latter. Yet we find them equally given to what is apparently indulgence. Lombroso has foolishly sought to find the source of this in madness — as if insanity could scale the peaks of Progress while Reason recoiled from the bergschrund. The explanation is far otherwise. Imagine to yourself the mental state of him who inherits or attains the full consciousness of the artist, that is to say, the divine consciousness.

He finds himself unutterably lonely, and he must steel himself to endure it. All his peers are dead long since! Even if he find an equal upon earth, there can scarcely be companionship, hardly more than the far courtesy of king to king. There are few twin souls in genius — rare even as twin stars.

Good — he can reconcile himself to the scorn of the world. But yet he feels with anguish his duty towards it. It is therefore essential to him to be human.

Now the divine consciousness is not full-flowered in youth. The newness of the objective world preoccupies the soul for many years. It is only as each illusion vanishes before the magic of the master that he gains more and more the power to dwell in the world of Reality. And with this comes the terrible temptation — the desire to enter and enjoy rather than remain among men and suffer their illusions. Yet, since the sole purpose of the incarnation of such Master was to help humanity, he must make the supreme renunciation. It is the problem of that dreadful bridge of Islam, Al Sirak; the razor-edge will cut the unwary foot, yet it must be trodden firmly, or the traveler will fall to the abyss. I dare not sit in the Old Absinthe House for ever, wrapped in the ineffable delight of the Beatific Vision. I must write this essay, that men may thereby come at last to understand true things. But the operation of the creative godhead is not enough. Art is itself too near the Reality which must be renounced for a season.

Therefore his work is also part of his temptation; the genius feels himself slipping constantly heavenward. The gravitation of eternity draws him. He is like a ship torn by the tempest from the harbour where the master must needs take on new passengers to the Happy Isles. So he must throw out anchors; and the only holding is the mire! Thus, in order to maintain the equilibrium of sanity, the artist is obliged to seek fellowship with the grossest of mankind. Like Lord Dunsany or Augustus John, today, or like Teniers of old, he may love to sit in taverns where sailors frequent; he may wander the country with gypsies, or he may form liaisons with the vilest men and women. Edward Fitzgerald would seek an illiterate fisherman, and spend weeks in his company; Verlaine made associates of Rimbaud and Bibi la Purée; Shakespeare consorted with the Earls of Pembroke and Southampton; Marlowe was actually killed during a brawl in a low tavern. And when we consider the sex-relation, it is hard to mention a genius who had a wife or mistress of even tolerable good character. If he had one, he would be sure to neglect her for a Vampire or a Shrew. A good woman is too near that heaven of Reality which he is sworn to renounce!

And this, I suppose, is why I am interested in the woman who has come to sit at the nearest table. Let us find out her story; let us try to see with the eyes of her soul!

V.

She is a woman of no more than thirty years of age, though she looks older. She comes here at irregular intervals, once a week or once a month; but when she comes she sits down to get solidly drunk on that alternation of beer and gin which the best authorities in England deem so efficacious.

As to her story, it is simplicity itself. She was kept in luxury for some years by a wealthy cotton broker, crossed to Europe with him, and lived in London and Paris like a queen. Then she got the idea of "respectability" and "settling down in life"; so she married a man who could keep her in mere comfort. Result: repentance, and a periodical need to forget her sorrows. She is still "respectable"; she never tires of repeating that she is not one of "those girls," but "a married woman living far up-town," and that she "never runs about with men."

It is not the failure of marriage; it is the failure of men to recognize what marriage was ordained to be. By a singular paradox, it is the triumph of the bourgeois, who is the chief supporter of marriage, that has degraded marriage to the level of the bourgeois. Only the hero is capable of marriage as the church understands it; for the marriage oath is a compact of appalling solemnity, an alliance of two souls against the world and against fate, with invocation of the great aid of the Most High. Death is not the most beautiful of adventures, as Charles Frohman said, on the "Titanic" ere she plunged, for death is unavoidable; marriage is a voluntary heroism. That marriage has today become a matter of convenience is the last word of the commercial spirit. It is as if one should take a vow of knighthood to combat dragons — until the dragons appeared.

So this poor woman, because she did not understand that respectability is a lie, that it is love that makes marriage sacred and not the sanction of church or state, because she took marriage as an asylum instead of as a crusade, has failed in life, and now seeks alcohol under the same fatal error. Wine is the ripe gladness which accompanies valor and rewards toil; it is the plume on a man's lance-head, a fluttering gallantry — not good to lean upon. Therefore her eyes are glassed with horror as she gazes uncomprehending upon her fate. That which she did all to avoid confronts her; she does not realize that, had she faced it, it would have fled with all the other phantoms. For the sole reality of this universe is God.

The Old Absinthe House is not a place; it is not bounded by four walls; it is headquarters of an army of philosophies. From this dim corner let me range, wafting thought through every air, salient against every problem of mankind; for it will always return like Noah's dove to this ark, this strange little sanctuary of the Green Goddess which has been set down not upon Ararat, but by the banks of the "Father of Waters."

VI.

Ah! the Green Goddess! What is the fascination that makes her so adorable and so terrible? Do you know that French sonnet *"La légende de l'absinthe?"* He must have loved it well, that poet.

What is there in absinthe that makes it a separate cult? The effects of its abuse are totally distinct from those of other stimulants. Even in ruin and in degradation it remains a thing apart; its victims wear a ghastly aureole all their own, and in their peculiar hell yet gloat with a sinister perversion of pride that they are not as other men.

But we are not to reckon up the uses of a thing by contemplating the wreckage of its abuse. We do not curse the sea because of occasional disasters to our mariners, or refuse axes to our woodsmen because we sympathize with Charles the First or Louis the Sixteenth. So therefore as special vices and dangers appertain to absinthe, so also do graces and virtues that adorn no other liquor.

The word is from the Greek apsinthion; it means "undrinkable" or, according to some authorities, "undelightful". In either case, strange paradox? No; for the wormwood draught itself were bitter beyond human endurance; it must be aromatized and mellowed with other herbs.

Chief among these is the gracious Melissa, of which the great Paracelsus thought so highly that he incorporated it as the chief ingredient in the preparation of his *Ens Melissa Vitae*, which he expected to be an elixir of life and a cure for all diseases, but which in his hands never came to perfection.

Then also there are added mint, anise, fennel and hyssop, all holy herbs familiar to all from the Treasury of Hebrew Scripture. And there is even the sacred marjoram which renders man both chaste and passionate; the tender green angelica stalks also infused in this most mystic of concoctions; for like the artemisia absinthium itself it is a plant of Diana, and gives the purity and lucidity, with a touch of the madness, of the Moon; and above all there is the Dittany of Crete of which the eastern Sages say that one flower hath more puissance in high magic than all the other gifts of all the gardens of the world. It is as if the first diviner of absinthe had been indeed a magician intent upon a combination of sacred drugs which should cleanse, fortify and perfume the human soul.

And it is no doubt that in the due employment of this liquor such effects are easy to obtain. A single glass seems to render the breathing freer, the spirit lighter, the heart more ardent, soul and mind alike more capable of executing the great task of doing that particular work in the world which the Father may have sent them to perform. Food itself loses its gross qualities in the presence of absinthe, and becomes even as manna, operating the sacrament of nutrition without bodily disturbance.

Let then the pilgrim enter reverently the shrine, and drink his absinthe as a stirrup-cup; for in the right conception of this life as an ordeal of chivalry lies the foundation of every perfection of philosophy. "Whatsoever ye do, whether ye eat or drink, do all to the glory of God!" applies with singular force to the absintheur. So may he come victorious from the battle of life to be received with tender kisses by some green-robed archangel, and crowned with mystic vervain in the Emerald Gateway of the Opal City of God.

VII.

And now the café is beginning to fill up. This little room with its dark green woodwork, its boarded ceiling, its sanded floor, its old pictures, its whole air of sympathy with time, is beginning to exert its magic spell. Here comes a curious child, short and sturdy, with a long blonde pigtail, her slave sly and sidelong on a jolly little old man who looks as if he had stepped straight out of the pages of Balzac.

Handsome and diminutive, with a fierce moustache almost as big as the rest of him, like a regular little Spanish fighting cock, Frank, the waiter, in his long white apron, struts to them with the glasses of ice-cold pleasure, green as the glaciers themselves. He will stand up bravely with the musicians by and by, and sing us a jolly song of old Catalonia.

The door swings open again; a tall dark girl, exquisitely slim and snaky, with masses of black hair knotted about her head, comes in; on her arm is a plump woman with hungry eyes, and a mass of Titian red hair. They seem distracted from the outer world, absorbed in some subject of enthralling interest; and they drink their apéritif as if in a dream. I ask the mulatto boy who waits at my table (the sleek and lithe black panther!) who they are; but he knows only that one is a cabaret dancer, the other the owner of a cotton plantation up river. At a round table in the middle of the room sits one of the proprietors with a group of friends; he is burly, rubicund, and jolly, the very type of the Shakespearian "Mine host." Now a party of a dozen merry boys and girls comes in; the old pianist begins to play a dance, and in a moment the whole café is caught up in the music of harmonious motion. Yet still the invisible line is drawn about each soul; the dance does not conflict with the absorption of the two strange women, or with my own mood of detachment.

Then there is a "little laughing lewd gamine" dressed all in black save for a square white collar; her smile is broad and free as the sun, and her gaze as clean and wholesome and inspiring. There is the big jolly blonde Irish girl in the black velvet béret and coat, and the white boots, chatting with two boys in khaki from the border; and there is the Creole girl in pure white capàpie, with her small piquant face and its round button of a nose, and its curious deep rose flush, and its red little mouth, impudently smiling. Around these islands seems to flow as a general tide the more stable life of the quarter. Here are honest goodwives seriously discussing their affairs, and heaven only knows if it be love or the price of sugar which engages them so wholly. There are but a few commonplace and uninteresting elements in the café; and these are without exception men. The giant Big Business is a great tyrant; he seizes all the men for slaves, and leaves the women to make shift as best they can for — all that makes life worth living. Candies and American Beauty Roses are of no use in an emergency! So, even in this most favored corner, there is dearth of the kind of men that women need.

At the table next to me sits an old, old man. He has done great things in his day, they tell me, an engineer, who first found it possible to dig Artesian wells in the Sahara desert. The Legion of Honor glows red in his shabby surtout. He comes here, one of the many wrecks of the Panama Canal, a piece of jetsam cast up by that tidal wave of speculation and corruption. He is of the old type, the thrifty peasantry; and he has his little income from the Rente. He says that he is too old to cross the ocean — and why should he, with the atmosphere of old France to be had a stone's throw from his little apartment in Bourbon Street? It is a curious type of house that one finds in this quarter in New Orleans; meagre without, within one comes unexpectedly upon great spaces, carved wooden balconies on which the rooms open. So he dreams away his honored days in the Old Absinthe House. His rusty black, with its worn red button, is a noble wear.

Black, by the way, seems almost universal among the women; is it instinctive good taste? At least, it serves to bring up the general level of good looks. Most American women spoil what little beauty they may have by overdressing. Here there is nothing extravagant, nothing vulgar, none of the near-Paris-gown and the just-off-Bond-Street hat. Nor is there a single dress to which a Quaker could object. There is neither the mediocrity nor the immodesty of the New York woman, who is tailored or millinered on a garish pattern, with the Eternal Chorus Girl as the Ideal — an ideal which she always attains, though (Heaven knows!) in "society" there are few "front-row" types.

On the other side of me a splendid stalwart maid, modern in muscle, old only in the subtle and modest fascination of her manner, her face proud, cruel and amorous, shakes her wild tresses of gold in pagan laughter. Her mood is universal as the wind. What can her cavalier be doing to keep her waiting? It is a little mystery which I will not solve for the reader; on the contrary ——

VIII.

Yes, it was my own sweetheart (no! not all the magazines can vulgarize that loveliest of words) who was waiting for me to be done with my musings. She comes in silently and stealthily, preening and purring like a great cat, and sits down, and begins to Enjoy. She knows I must never be disturbed until I close my pen. We shall go together to dine at a little Italian restaurant kept by an old navy man, who makes the best ravioli this side of Genoa; then we shall walk the wet and windy streets, rejoicing to feel the warm subtropical rain upon our faces; we shall go down to the Mississippi, and watch the lights of the ships, and listen to the tales of travel and adventure of the mariners. There is one that moves me greatly; it is like the story of the sentinel of Herculaneum. A cruiser of the U. S. Navy was detailed to Rio de Janeiro. (This was before the days of wireless telegraphy.) The port was in quarantine; the ship had to stand ten miles out to sea. Nevertheless Yellow Jack managed to come aboard. The men died one by one. There was no way of getting word to Washington; and, as it turned out later, the Navy Department had completely forgotten the existence of the ship. No orders came; the captain stuck to his post for three months. Three months of solitude and death! At last a passing ship was signalled, and the cruiser was moved to happier waters. No doubt the story is a lie; but did that make it less splendid in the telling, as the old scoundrel sat and spat and chewed tobacco? No, we will certainly go down, and ruffle it on the wharves. There is really better fun in life than can be got by going to the movies, when you know how to make terms with Reality.

There is beauty in every incident of life; the true and the false, the wise and the foolish, are all one in the eye that beholds all without passion or prejudice; and the secret appears to lie not in the retirement from the world, but in keeping a part of oneself Vestal, sacred, impact, aloof from that self which makes contact with the external universe; in other words, in a separation of that which is and perceives from that which acts and suffers. And the art of doing this is really the art of being an artist. As a rule, it is a birthright; it may perhaps be attained by prayer and fasting; most surely, it can never be bought.

But if you have it not, this will be the best way to get it — or something like it. Give up your life completely to the task; sit daily for six hours in the Old Absinthe House, and sip the icy opal; endure till all things change insensibly before your eyes, you changing with them; till you become as gods, knowing good and evil, and this also — that they are not two but one.

It may be a long time before the veil lifts; but a moment's experience of the point of view of the artist is worth a myriad martyrdoms. It solves every problem of life and of death — which two also are one.

It translates this universe into intelligible terms, relating truly the ego with the non-ego, and recasting the prose of reason in the poetry of soul. Even as the eye of the sculptor beholds his masterpiece already existing in the shapeless mass of marble, needing only the loving-kindness of the chisel to cut away the veils of Isis, so you may (perhaps) learn to behold the sum and summit of all grace and glory from this great observatory, the Old Absinthe House of New Orleans.

Liber Porta Lucis

I behold a small dark orb, wheeling in an abyss of infinite space. It is minute among a myriad vast ones, dark amid a myriad bright ones.

I who comprehend in myself all the vast and the minute, all the bright and the dark, have mitigated the brilliance of mine unutterable splendour, sending forth V.V.V.V.V. as a ray of my light, as a messenger unto that small dark orb.

Then V.V.V.V.V. taketh up the word, and sayeth:

Men and women of the Earth, to you am I come from the Ages beyond the Ages, from the Space beyond your vision; and I bring to you these words.

But they heard him not, for they were not ready to receive them.

But certain men heard and understood, and through them shall this Knowledge be made known.

The least therefore of them, the servant of them all, writeth this book.

He writeth for them that are ready. Thus is it known if one be ready, if he be endowed with certain gifts, if he be fitted by birth, or by wealth, or by intelligence, or by some other manifest sign. And the servants of the master by his insight shall judge of these.

This Knowledge is not for all men; few indeed are called, but of these few many are chosen.

This is the nature of the Work.

First, there are many and diverse conditions of life upon this earth. In all of these is some seed of sorrow. Who can escape from sickness and from old age and from death?

We are come to save our fellows from these things. For there is a life intense with knowledge and extreme bliss which is untouched by any of them.

To this life we attain even here and now. The adepts, the servants of V.V.V.V.V., have attained thereunto.

It is impossible to tell you of the splendours of that to which they have attained. Little by little, as your eyes grow stronger, will we unveil to you the ineffable glory of the Path of the Adepts, and its nameless goal.

Even as a man ascending a steep mountain is lost to sight of his friends in the valley, so must the adept seem. They shall say: He is lost in the clouds. But he shall rejoice in the sunlight above them, and come to the eternal snows.

Or as a scholar may learn some secret language of the ancients, his friends shall say: "Look! he pretends to read this book. But it is unintelligible --- it is nonsense." Yet he delights in the Odyssey, while they read vain and vulgar things.

We shall bring you to Absolute Truth, Absolute Light, Absolute Bliss.

Many adepts throughout the ages have sought to do this; but their words have been perverted by their successors, and again and again the Veil has fallen upon the Holy of Holies.

To you who yet wander in the Court of the Profane we cannot yet reveal all; but you will easily understand that the religions of the world are but symbols and veils of the Absolute Truth. So also are the philosophies. To the adept, seeing all these things from above, there seems nothing to choose between Buddha and Mohammed, between Atheism and Theism.

The many change and pass; the one remains. Even as wood and coal and iron burn up together in one great flame, if only that furnace be of transcendent heat; so in the alembic of this spiritual alchemy, if only the zelator blow sufficiently upon his furnace all the systems of earth are consumed in the One Knowledge.

Nevertheless, as a fire cannot be started with iron alone, in the beginning one system may be suited for one seeker, another for another.

We therefore who are without the chains of ignorance, look closely into the heart of the seeker and lead him by the path which is best suited to his nature unto the ultimate end of all things, the supreme realization, the Life which abideth in Light, yea, the Life which abideth in Light.

Apollo Bestows the Violin
A Story For the Stage
Part I

The pastureland reached from the border of the olives and figs that garlanded the village to the upper slopes of the mountain, whose tumbled rocks, fire-scarred, frowned the menace of eternal sterility, the Universe against struggling man.

It was not often that Daphnis led his goats too far toward the crags, for the plain was green and gracious. Only in one spot was the sward broken. There did mosses and flowers, yellow, blue, and white, cover a mound as soft and firm as a maiden's breast.

Daphnis, true child, loved to make believe that this mound was sacred to some nymph. He would never invade the circle, or allow his goats to wander on it. But he would take his flute and invoke the nymph, or express the faint stirrings of manhood in his boyish breast by some such simple song as this:

> "Goats of mine, give ear, give ear!
> Shun this mound for food or frolic!
> Heaven is open; gods are near
> To my musings melancholic.
> Spring upon the earth begets
> Daffodils and violets.

> Here it was maybe that Zeus
> With his favourite took his pleasure;
> Here maybe the Satyrs use
> With the nymphs tread a measure.
> Let no wanton foot distress
> This encircled loveliness!
>
> Oh, some destined nymph may deign
> Through the lilies to come gliding,
> Snatch from earth the choral swain,
> Hold him in her breast in hiding!
> See, they stir. It is the wind:
> Of my case they have no mind."

Thus lamenting and complaining the days found him, a monotony pastoral whose cycle was but peace.

But on the day of the summer solstice, as he plainted with the old refrain, the lilies stirred more violently; and the day was windless. Also it seemed to him as if a faint mist inhabited their midst. And he sang: ---

> "Mist, is this the fairy veil
> Of the bright one that's for me?
> Too phantastic, false and frail,
> See, it melts to vanity!"

Yet was he eagerly afoot with curiosity, for now the mist rose in fiercer puffs, and little jets of flame spurted and sparkled amid the lilies: ---

"Is the earth herself (he sang) that breathes
In the bosom of the flowers?
Is it fatal fire that seethes
From the heart of hateful powers?"

And the tumult of the mound increasing ever, he went forward a step toward the circle; yet again his self-set fear caught him, and he drew back --- yet again his eagerness lured him. In the end, reality conquered imagination; he advanced delicately up the knoll.

Like the nipple of a breast, earth protruded, red, puckered, fissured. This Daphnis saw as he broke through the tall lilies. From its centre jetted the dusky, rose-red mist. As he thrust forward his arms to divide the flowers, the breeze caught a curl of smoke and mixed it with his breath.

His head went back: he half choked. Then a strangled cry broke from him, turning to wild laughter. His limbs caught the craze. He leapt and twirled and pirouetted like one stung by a tarantula: and all the while meaningless cries issued from his throat.

The nearer he approached the nipple the more fantastic were his antics, the more strident his laughter.

Now at the foot of the mound appeared a company of merchants and slaves journeying in caravan. All these, attracted from their path by the unwonted sounds, beheld him thus dancing. The whisper went round: "He is possessed of the spirit of some God," and they all fell upon their faces and worshipped.

Then followed the wonder of all; for at high noon was the sun wrapped in blackness of eclipse. In the gathering darkness and the strange shadows Daphnis still leapt and laughed; but as the sun was wholly swallowed by the dragon, he gave one supreme shriek, and fell exhausted.

Part II

That which had been a mound of flowers was hidden deep beneath a floor of marble, translucent as mother-of-pearl. Along each side four elephants of obsidian, crouching, did homage to the central object of the hall, a slim tripod of silver, and on their backs eight pillars of porphyry were swathed with pythons of gold and black. These supported the dome, which glittered with lapis-lazuli. The shape of the temple was that of a fish or vesica, and nowhere was there any cross or tau to be seen.

Beneath the tripod a circular hole in the marble admitted the dusky vapours which two centuries before had filled Daphnis with enthusiasm.

Beyond and between each elephant stood five priestesses in white robes, their faces wrapped closely even to the eyes, lest the fumes should cause them to fall into trance. Each of these held in her hand a torch filled with oil pressed from the sacred olives that grew in the groves of the temple, and each was blind and deaf from too long continuance in the shrine whose glory was so dazzling and whose music so intense. Each might have been a statue of snow at some antique revery of a Tsar.

Beyond the last of these, where the temple narrowed, was a shrine hidden, for from the roof hung a veil of purple, on which were written in golden letters the names and titles of Apollo.

It was the hour of worship; with uplifted hands a bearded priest in a voluminous robe of azure and gold cried aloud the invocations. He stood beyond the tripod, his face toward the shrine.

> "Hail to the Lord of the Sun!
> Mystic, magnificent one!
> Who shall contend with him? None.
> Hail to the Lord of the Sun!
> Hail to the Lord of the Bow!
> He hath chosen an arrow, and lo!
> Shall any avail with him? No!
> Hail to the Lord of the Bow!"

And then turning towards the tripod: ---

> "Hail to the Lord of the Lyre!
> Diviner of death and desire,
> Prophetic of favour and fire,
> Hail to the Lord of the Lyre!"

With this he turned again and went up to the veil, prostrating himself seven times. Then again he turned and came to the tripod and sang: ---

> "Prophetess, pythoness, hear!
> Child of Apollo, descend!

Smooth from the soul of the sphere
Of the sun, be upon us, befriend!
In the soothsaying smoke of the hollow
Do thou and thine oracle follow
The word and the will of Apollo!"

So saying, he cast incense upon the opening beneath the tripod, and retired into the shrine. As the smoke cleared, there was found seated upon the tripod a maiden in a close fitting dress of crimson silk broidered with gold. Her masses of black hair, caught at the crown with a fillet of crimson and gold, fell heavily around her. She bore a lyre in her hands. Her eyes were wild and fierce, and she sniffed up the vapours of the cavern with awesome ardour. Feebly at first, afterwards frenetically, she plucked at the strings.

Hardly a minute --- a string snapped; the whole music jarred; and the priest ran from the shrine, shrieking "Apollo! Apollo! Veil your faces! Apollo hath descended." Himself he flung upon the marble before the tripod. There was a noise as of thunder; the veil was swept open as by a whirlwind, and Apollo, one flame of gold, entered the temple. As he passed, the priestesses fell dead and their torches were extinct. But a ray of glory from above, a monstrance to the God, followed him. Slowly and majestically he moved to the tripod. In his hands he bore an instrument of wood, of unfamiliar shape. Music of triumph and of glory answered his paces.

To the pythoness he advanced, thus dancing. He took the lyre from her hands and broke it. She stared, entranced. He put the strange instrument into her hands and, drawing down her head, pressed his lips to her forehead. Then he breathed lightly on her hands. Darkness fell, and lightnings rent it; thunders answered them. Apollo was gone. After the thunder the temple was filled with rosy radiance. The old priest, still prone, raised and let fall his hands, in mechanical imitation of the signs of invocation. Obedient, the pythoness began to play upon the instrument given of the God, and the temple shuddered at sounds so ethereal, so soul shaking, so divine. A greater music had been given to the world.

She ended. The old priest rose unsteadily to his feet, crying: "Apollo! Apollo!" staggered, and fell dead before the tripod.

The light went out.

The Soul of the Desert

Dedicated to Soror Alta Via
one who lives on the desert

"I too am the Soul of the Desert; thou shalt seek me yet again in the wilderness of sand."

Part 1:
The Journey

The soul is, in its own nature, perfect purity, perfect calm, perfect silence; and as a well springs from the very veins of the earth itself, so is the soul nurtured of the blood of God, the ecstasy of things.

This soul can never be injured, never marred, never defiled. Yet all things added to it do for a time trouble it; and this is sorrow.

To this, language itself bears witness; for all words which mean unhappy mean first of all disturbed, disquieted, troubled. The root idea of sorrow is this idea of stirring up.

For many a year man in his quest for happiness has travelled a false road. To quench his thirst he has added salt in ever increasing quantities to the water of life; to cover the ant heaps of his imagination he has raised mountains wherein wild beasts and deadly prowl. To cure the itch, he has flayed the patient; to exorcise the ghost, he has evoked the devil.

It is the main problem of philosophy, how this began. The Rishis, seven that sat on Mount Kailasha and considered thus, answered that the soul became self-conscious; and crying, "I am That!" became two even in the act of asserting it was One. This theory may be found not too remote from truth by whoso returns to that tower upon the ramparts of the soul and beholds the city.

But let us leave it to the doctors to discuss the cause of the malady; for the patients it is enough to know the cure and take it. Abana and Pharpar, rivers of Damascus, are not worth the simplicity of Jordan. The prophet has spoken; it is our concern now to obey: and so sweet and so full of virtue are these waters that the first touch thrills the soul with the sure foretaste of its cure.

Doubt not, brother! Reason indeed may elaborate complexities; are not these the very symptoms of the disease? Use but the rude common sense, heritage of simpler and happier forefathers, that they have transmitted to thee by the wand.

The cure of disease is ease; of disquiet, quiet; of strife, peace. And to attain horsemanship the study of folios aids not, but the mounting of a horse; as the best way to swim is to enter the water and strike out, so it is cool sense, not feverish reason, that says: to attain quiet, practice quiet.

There are men so strong of will, so able to concentrate the mind, to neglect the impressions that they do not wish to receive, that they can withdraw themselves from their surroundings, even when those are as multitudinous and insistent as those of a great city. But for the most part of men, it is best to begin in easier circumstances, to climb the mountain in fine weather before attacking it in the snowstorm.

And yet the eager aspirant will answer: Provided that the cure is complete. Provided that the sickness does not return when the medicine is stopped.

Ah! that were hard: so deepseated is the malady that years after its symptoms have passed, it seizes on a moment of weakness to blaze out again. It is malarial fever that lurks low, that hides in the very substance of the blood itself, that has made the very fountain of life partaker with it in the sacrament of death.

"Has a spider found out the communion cup?"

"Was a toad in the christening font?"

No: the remedy cures surely enough; but not often does it cure once for all, beyond relapse. But it is simple; once the symptoms have properly abated, they never return with equal force; and if the patient has but the wit to stretch out the hand for another dose, the fever dies.

What is then the essential? To cure the patient once; to give him faith in the efficacy of the remedy, so that perchance he falls sick, and no doctor is near, he may be able to cure himself.

If Thought then be that which troubles the soul, there is but one way to take. Stop thinking.

It is the most difficult task that man can undertake. "Give me a fulcrum for my lever," said Archimedes, "and I will move the earth." But how, when one is within, and part of, that very system of motion which one had desired to stop? Newton's first law drops like the headsman's axe on the very name of our endeavor. Well for us that this is not true as it is obvious! For this fact saves us, that the resolution of all these is rest. The motion is but in reciprocal pairs; the sum of its vectors is zero. The knot of the Universe is a fool's knot; for all it seems Gordian, pull but firmly, and it ravels out. It is this seeming that is all the mischief; gloomy is the gulf, and the clouds gather angrily in monstrous shapes; the false moon flickers behind them; abyss upon abyss opens on every hand. Darkness and menace; the fierce sound of hostile things!

One glimmer of starlight, and behold the golden bridge! Narrow and straight, keen as the razor's edge and glittering as the sword's blade, a proper bridge if thou leanest not to right or left. Cross it — good! but all this is in the dream. Wake! Thou shalt know that all together, gulf, moon, bridge, dragon and the rest, were but the phantasms of sleep howbeit, remember this, that to cross the bridge in sleep is the only way to waking.

I do not know if many men have the same experience as myself in the matter of voluntary dreaming, or rather of contest between the sought and the unsought in dream. For instance, I am on a ridge of ice with Oscar Eckenstein. He slips to one side. I throw myself on the other. We begin to cut steps up to the ridge; my axe snaps, or is snatched from my hand. We begin to pull ourselves up to the ridge by the rope; the rope begins to fray. Luckily it is caught lower down on a cleft of rock. A Lammergeier swoops; I invent a pistol and blow its brains out. And so on through a thousand adventures, making myself master of each event as it arises. But I am grown old today and weary of thrills. Nowadays at the first hint of danger I take wing and sail majestically down to the glacier.

If I have thus digressed, it is to superimpose this triangle on that of the task, "Stop Thinking." Simple it sounds, and simple it is — when you have mastery. In the meantime it is apt to lead you far indeed from simplicity. I have myself written some million words in order to stop thinking! I have covered miles of canvas with pounds of paint in order to stop thinking. Thus may it be that I am at least to be considered as no mean authority on all the wrong ways; and so perhaps, by a process of exclusion, on the right way!

Unfortunately, it is not as easy is this: . . . .

There are nine and sixty ways of constructing tribal lays.

And every single one of them is right.

And right for A is often wrong for B.

But, luckily, the simpler the goal is kept, the simpler are the means. Elsewhere in my writings will be found a fairly painstaking and accurate account of the process. The present essay is but to advocate a mighty engine adjuvant — the shoulder of Hercules to the cartwheel of the beginner whose diffidence whispers that he is incapable of following those instructions in the difficult circumstances of ordinary life, or for the enthusiast who wisely determines like Kirkpatrick to "mak siccar." Indeed, the cares of this world, the deceitfulness of the riches, the lusts of the flesh and the eye, the pride of life, and all the other enemies of the saint, do indeed choke the word, and it becometh unfruitful.

Part 2:
The Desert

As a monastery imposes the false peace of dullness by its unwholesome and artificial monotony, so is the desert nature's own cure for all the tribulations of thought.

There the soul undergoes a triplex weaving. First, the newness of the surroundings, their strange and salient simplicity, charm the soul. It has a premonition of its cure; it feels the atmosphere of home. It is sure of its vocation. Next, the mind, its frivolity once satiate with novelty, becomes bored, turns to acrimony, even to passionate revolt. The novice beats against the bars; the stranger to the desert flies to London or to Paris with the devil at his heels. A wise superior will not restrain the acolyte who cannot restrain himself; but in the desert, the refugee, if he doubts his own powers — still more, maybe, if he does not mistrust them! — would wisely make it impossible to return. But how should he do so? Believe me, who have tried it, the longest journey, the most bitter hardships, are as nothing, an arrow-light of joy, when the great horror lies behind and the sanctuary of Paris ahead!

For, indeed, this is the great horror, solitude, when the soul can no longer bathe in the ever-changing mind, laugh as its sunlit ripples lap its skin, but, shut up in the castle of a few thoughts, paces its narrow prison, wearing down the stone of time, feeding on its own excrement. There is no star in the blackness of that night, no foam upon the stagnant and putrid sea. Even the glittering health that the desert brings to the body is like a spear in the soul's throat. The passionate ache to act, to think: this eats into the soul like a cancer. It is the scorpion striking itself in its agony, save that no poison can add to the torture of the circling fire, no superflux of anguish relieve it by annihilation. But against these paroxysms is an eightfold sedative. The ravings of madness are lost in soundless space; the struggles of the drowning man are not heeded by the sea.

These are the eight genii of the desert. They are the eight Elements of Fohi:

Male: The Lingam (Life), The Sun, Fire, Air (Wood)

Female: The Yoni (Space, The Stars), The Moon, Water, Earth

In the desert all these are single; all these are naked. They are pure and untroubled; not breaking up and dissolving by any commingling or communion; each remains itself and apart, harmonizing indeed with its fellows, but in no wise interfering. The lines of demarcation are crude and harsh; but softness is incomprehensibly the result. They are immitigable, these Eight Elements, and together they mitigate immeasurably. The mind that revolts against them is ground down by their persistent careless pressure. It is as when one throws a crystal — say of microscopic salt — into water: it is eaten silently and rapidly, and is no more; the water is untroubled always; its action is like Fate's, infinitely irresistible yet infinitely calm.

So the mind reaches out to think this or think that; it is brought back into silence by the eight great facts. The desert wind suffers no obstacle to impede it; the sun shines invincibly upon the baked earth of the village; the sand invisibly eats up the oasis, save for a moment where man casts up his earthworks against it. Yet despite this, the spring leaps unexpected from the sand, and no simoon can stifle, nor even evaporate it; nor can the immense sterility of the desert conquer life. Look where you will, every dune of sand has its inhabitants — not colonists, but natives of the inhospitable-seeming waste. The moon itself, serenely revolving around earth, changes in appearance, as if to say: "Even so goest thou about the sun. Am I new or full? Never think of it; that is but the point of view from which thou chancest to regard me. I am but a mirror of sunlight, dark or bright according to the angle of thy gaze. Does the mirror alter? Is it not always the untroubled silver? Have not I always one face turned sunward? Thou but mockest thyself if thou call me 'The Changeful.'"

With such reflections or their kin, it may be, shalt thou make an end of the revolt of the mind against the desert.

For life itself, here in the oasis, is a thing ordered by these elements. Night is for sleep; there is nothing whereat to wake. There is no artificial light; no artificial food — literature. There is no choice of meats; one is always hungry. The desert sauce is hunger unique as the Englishman's one sauce. Having eaten, one must walk; there is only one place to walk in. There is only one lesson to learn, peace; only one comment upon the lesson, thanksgiving. Love itself becomes simple as the rest of life. A glance in the Café Maure, a silent agreement with delight, a soft withdrawal to some hollow of the dunes under the stars where the village is blotted out as though it had never been, as are in that happy moment all the transgressions of the sinner, and all the woes of life, but the Virtue of the Holy One; or else to some dim corner of a garden of the oasis by the stream, where through the softly stirring palms strikes the first moon-ray from the East, and life thrills in sleepy unison; all, all in silence, no names or vows exchanged, but with clean will an act accomplished. No more. No turmoil, no confusion, no despair, no self-tormenting, hardly even a memory.

And this too at first is horrible; one expects so much from love, three volumes of falsehood, a labyrinth rather than a garden. It is hard at first to realize that this is no more love than a carbuncle is part of a man's neck. All the spices wherewith we are wont to season the dish to our depraved palates, Maxim's, St. Margaret's, automobile rides, the Divorce Court, these are unwholesome pleasures. They are not love. Nor is love the exaltation of emotions, sentiment, follies. The stage door is not love (nor is the stile in Lovers' Lane); love is the bodily ecstasy of dissolution, the pang of bodily death, wherein the Ego for a moment that is an eon loses the fatal consciousness of itself; and becoming one with that of another, foreshadows to itself that greater sacrament of death, when "the spirit returns to God that gave it."

And this secret has also its part in the economy of life. By the road of silence one comes to the gate of the City of God. As the mind is the warring might (that is peace unshakeable) of these Eight Elements of the Desert, so at last the Ego is found alone, unmasked, conscious of itself and of no other thing. This is the supreme anguish of the soul; it realizes itself as itself, as a thing separate from that which is not itself, from God. In this spasm there are two ways: if fear and pride are left in the soul, it shuts itself up, like a warlock in a tower, gnashing its teeth with agony. "I am I," it cries, "I will not lose myself," and in that state damned, it is slowly torn by the claws of circumstance, disintegrated bitterly, for all its struggles, throughout ages and ages, its rags to be cast piecemeal upon the dungheap without the city. But the soul that has understood the blessedness of that resignation, which grasps the universe and devours it, which is without hope or fear, without faith or doubt, without hate or love, dissolves itself ineffable into the abounding bliss of God. It cries with Shelley, as the "chains of lead about its flight of fire" drop molten from its limbs: "I pant, I sink, I tremble, I expire," and in that last outbreaking is made one with the primal and final breath, the Holy Spirit of God.

Such must be the climax of any retirement to the Desert on the part of any aspirant of the Mysteries who has the spark of that fire in him.

He is drawn to physical quiescence (to regularity, simplicity, unity of motion) by the constant example and compulsion of the Elements. He is obliged to introspection by the poverty of exterior impression, perceptions behind the sensations, the laws underlying even the perception, and finally that consciousness which is the lawgiver. Sooner or later, according to his energy and the sanctification of his will, must he tear down the great veil and behold himself upon the shining walls of space, must he utter with shuddering rapture: "This is I!" Then let him choose!

From this moment of the annihilation of the Self in Pan, he is cured of the disease, "self-knowledge." He may return among his fellows, and move among them as a king, shine among them as a star. To him will they turn insensibly for light; to him will they come for the healing of their wounds.

He shall lift up the sacred Lance, and touch therewith the side of the king that was wounded by no lesser weapon; and the king shall be healed.

He shall plunge the point of the Lance into the Holy Grail, and it shall again glow with life and ecstasy, giving forth its bounty of mysterious refreshment to all the company of knights.

Then, should the rocks of life tear him, and its snow chill him, knoweth he not where to turn? Hath he not attained the secret? Hath he not entered into the Sanctuary of the Most High?

Is he not chosen and armed against all things? Is he not master of Destiny and of the Event? What can touch him, who hath become intangible, being lost in God? Or conquer him, who hath become unconquerable, having conquered himself and given himself up to God? As well write upon the sand, as write sorrow in his soul. As well seek to darken the Sun, as to put out the Light that is in him.

Thus I wrote in the palm gardens of Tozeur, by the waters of its spring; thus I wrote while the sun moved mightily down the sky, and the wind whispered that it came no whence and went no whither, even as it listed from everlasting to everlasting.

Amen

Tozeur
17 March 1914

The Opium-Smoker
(in eight fugues)

I

Crown me with poppy-leaves: sere are the bays.
Fling down the myrtle: the myrtle decays.
Still be the strife of the strenuous days!

Still be thy stridency, Player Pandean!
Soothe me the lute; but oh hush to the pean!
Feed me on kisses of flowers Lethean!

Specks on the wheel are the nights and the days,
Fast as they fall from me, lost in the haze,
Sobered to softness of silvery grays.

Satan is fallen from the pale empyrean
Down in the dusk with the dead Galilean:—
Fill me the cup of the poppy Circean!

II

Hardly a glimmer to chasten the gloom;
Hardly a murmur of Time at his loom;
Nothing of sense but the poppy-perfume.

Boy, as you love me, I charge you to fold
Pipe over pipe into gardens of gold

Such as a god may be glad to behold.

Seated on high in the eons of doom,
Sucked as a seed to the infinite womb,
Sealed is my soul in the sheath of its tomb.

Boy, as you love me, I charge you to mould
Pipe after pipe, till the heavens are rolled
Back and are lost as a tale that is told!

III

Silence and darkness are weaving a web
Broidered with Nothing at uttermost ebb:—
Cover, oh cover the shaming of Seb!

Fling the wide veil, O Nuit, on the shame!—
Shame from the Knowledge and unto the Name—
Hide it, O hide it, in flowers of flame!

Now in the balance of infinite things
Stirs not a feather; the universe swings
Poised on the stealth of ineffable wings.

Surely the sable Osirian bird
Sole in the ether shall utter the Word
Now that its crying can never be heard!

IV

See how the Star of the Universe blazes!
Millions of meteors in marvellous mazes
Mingle their magic of peony praises.

Oh! the dark streak on the heart of its flood!
Smitten is the Star, and its poisonous blood
Drips through the race of the luminous scud.

Poison and poison and poison! I quiver,
Drenched with the hate of the horrible river—
O but the stars of it stagger and shiver!

Leave me in peace, O disaster of light!
Leave me to solitude, leave me to night!
Is there no moon to enkindle the height?

V

See how the moon with her amrita dews
Drinks up the death of the Star, and renews
Life in cascades of peonian hues!

Nay, but she curves to arise, to increase;
Glamour on glamour to sicken and cease.
How shall the warrior win to the peace?

Fade, O thou moon in thy magical bark!
Sink in the ocean thy silvery spark!
Leave me, ah leave me alone in the dark!

Art thou not burnt in the fire of my will?
See, by the flashes that crimson and kill
I am the master; the magic is still.

VI

See! how the wrath of my rune that I send her,
Fire of my fire, is flung flying to end her,
Wrapping in ruin that scintillant splendour.

Fire of my fire! how the brilliance darts forth,
Runs to the uttermost pole of the north,
Splashing all space with the spume of my wrath!

Ah! but the subtle, the perilous way;
That hath no fire to enkindle the clay.
Ever to all be the work of me Nay!

I who am Being and Knowledge and Bliss
Lack by so much of the utter abyss :—
Bring me, O bring me, O bring me to this !

VII

Nay! it is over; I may not attain.
Why am I faint but because I am fain
Roll me the rapture of amber again!

Ah! but the poppy's deciduous dream
May not avail me to stand to the stream

Bearing me back from the Mighty Extreme.

Subtle and sombre the eagre of sleep
Rolls up the bay to envelope the steep.
What then is left, what is left—but to weep?

Maybe the stridency purpled of Pan
Leads at the last to the light of His plan.
Maybe his work is the wealth of a man!

VIII

Bring me the tablets, the stylus of jade!
Lend me thy light, O compassionate maid!
Soul of the master, O come to mine aid!

Make me the man of the marvellous mission!
Sharpen the sword of veridical vision
Cut me the knot of the mighty magician!

Here I devote me (record me the vow)
Unto the terrible task of the Tao.
Soul of the master, the writer be thou!

Bring me the tablets and stylus! Have done!
Guard me the doors; they are open to none,
Not to the Emperor! I have begun.

Baphomet

A black two-headed Eagle is GOD; even a Black Triangle is He. In His claws He beareth a sword; yea, a sharp sword is held therein.

This Eagle is burnt up in the Great Fire; yet not a feather is scorched. This Eagle is swallowed up in the Great Sea; yet not a feather is wetted. So flieth He in the air, and lighteth upon the earth at His pleasure.

So spake JACOBUS BURGUNDUS MOLENSIS the Grand Master of the Temple; and of the GOD that is Ass-headed did he dare not speak.

The Drug
I

I never suspected that my quiet friend was a wizard. Until that fatal Sunday afternoon I had always supposed that the little black door was a cupboard. This was the way of it.

It had long been my habit to spend Sunday with my quiet friend. I believe in Sunday as the Day of Rest, and the British Sunday is usually the acme of restless misery. But in my friend's house and its quiet park the wheels of the week went round smoothly. Especially so in the little observatory which he had built over the lake. It had no door upon the landward side, but a quay ran within it and beneath, so that (entering by boat) one found oneself at the foot of a small spiral staircase, narrow and dark, which led one out into a bright room, windowed on every side, at a height of nearly fifty feet from the water. So large and lofty was the room, so narrow seemed the tower, that I may surely be excused for having thought that the little black door in the East was but a shallow cupboard.

Many a Sunday had passed pleasantly within this room. Now we would read, now play chess or cards; or now he would play upon the violin, when our morning's sport among the trout was over. It was our custom to broil the fish over a clear fire, and to eat it with bread and the fruit of his beautiful orchards, while certain goodly vintages refreshed us with their subtle enthusiasm.

I should like you to picture my friend. He was still young, pale and slim, with a certain remote beauty dwelling lively on his cheeks, deep in his eyes. He was quiet as few men are quiet, yet every gesture glittered with starry joy.

His quiet, indeed, was the twinkling of the stars.

Upon this fatal Sunday afternoon, as we played chess together, I noticed thrice that his attention wandered to the clock with grave enquiry.

So preoccupied, indeed, was he that the game languished, and he agreed to a draw. "Will you forgive me," he said, "for a moment if I leave you? As you know, I dabble slightly in chemistry, and an important operation awaits a particular instant of time this afternoon. Stay!" he added, "why should you not become (as Kelly says) 'partaker of the mysteries of the creation'?"

Thus saying, he opened the door—the little black door—with a key (for it had no handle), and I beheld a curious apartment built in the thickness of the wall.

Very long, very narrow, very lofty; its walls of dead black. At one end hung in the midst a tall, slim tube of pale violet—a film of fire in whose light we seemed colouress spectres.

On the walls were shelves full of strange apparatus, mostly of glass or—as it seemed—silver.

My quiet friend executed some intricate movements with deft elegance.

Enough!" he smiled—" 'twas but a moment's work, yet many a month have I had to wait for the right instant."

I had no idea," said I, "that so strange a laboratory existed."

The products," he answered, "are in keeping. Look at this flask!"

'Twas a queer twisted shape, greenish with gold flecks—something not inhuman perhaps; something sinuous and serpentine, beyond doubt.

This liquor," he continued, as we moved back into the other room, "is made by taking pure mercury and exposing it in a certain manner to the action of the sun and of the air. The fire then passes over it and it is ready to receive the influence of the constellation of Virgo, and of Saturn the planet. Thus it grows exceeding dark—yet at the end? Behold!"

He placed a drop upon the palm of his hand. 'Twas a drop of purest opal, flashing with many tints, self-luminous. A light smoke floated up from it into the still air: a moment, and it was vanished altogether.

'Tis a volatile drug!" explained my friend; "even now I am at work up on it, that I may fix it. But the task is passing hard."

What is its name?" I asked.

Surely you are not one of those who think that by naming aught they have explained it! Suffice it," he added, "that all men drink once of this drug, but no man twice!"

Then," I laughed, "the name of it must be Death."

No!" he smiled, "I think not. Come, drink, my friend! It is the drug that giveth strange vision."

He poured about a drachm of the fluid into a tall glass. Its appearance was quite altered, being now of a grey pearly sheen.

Drink!" he cried, "drink!"

I lifted the glass and drank. Its taste was subtle and sweet as a kiss is; an ecstasy woke in me for an instant. Then I sank down, out of things, into a rich red gloom that grew blacker and blacker. Meseems that much time passed; but who can measure the time of a consciousness that is but the negation of all things?

Yet was I content in annihilation and—as it seemed—at rest.

II

Quite suddenly consciousness returned. I was muffled in black night, suffocated by darkness, awake to a strange nameless fear.

Hardly was I aware of this when from all sides came upon me an agonising pressure, like the frenzied grip of some giant hand. Even as my bones crushed beneath it, it relaxed. But my peace was gone; I was disturbed, anxious; I waited.

Not in vain. Again and again came the clutch upon me, each time more terrible than the last.

'Twas all so meaningless—I never guessed—how could I guess?

Also I tried to struggle and to shriek. Useless; my voice seemed gone.

Then—ah God! one spasm of steel ten thousand times fiercer than all the rest—a blaze of light in my eyes—and a wail of helpless agony, as it were, crushed out of me, that turned into a shrill scream of pain—of pain—unspeakable—unthinkable—I cannot bear to write of it.

Then a long lull.

A certain animal content, reaction from the agony.

A certain animal discontent, echo of the agony.

And dawning vistas of strange visions.

Of strange, strange visions.

Vast was the concave of the orb of light wherein I found myself. The light was of a cool, earthy green filtered through dew and reflected by flowers. A soft alluring scent was in the air; and a ripple as of slow invisible waters.

A tide of happiness and expectation played in my soul like the wind in the branches of an oak, making delicious music. Yet still there came now and again swift, strange pangs memorial of that past agony, and sudden fits of weeping shook me. But, one dream with another, the scene was inexpressly delightful.

The sole avenue open to the forces of mental discomfort was the budding sense of insecurity. Pleasures and pains alike had no obvious source; their function and purpose were still more obscure. The question even arose: Are all the phenomena detached? Or, in a word, am I insane?

The stress of this particular anxiety was increased by the alluring paths of research that opened to me. As vision after vision passed in fleeting rapture over my gaze, I seemed to grasp a certain shadowy nexus; then would arise another in the light of which the whole grouping broke down.

It seems trifling; you would hardly believe the mental agony that this simple matter caused; and—now— rose ever the mocking query: Insane?

However, as I became more used to the scene, certain facts did become clearer. The faint greenish luminosity was certainly due to the concourse of bright stars that hung in the limpid, colourless ether. One of these stars would now and again come dropping through the sky, and each, as it dropped, would burst into flame, shaped into some strange vision which riveted my attention. It would perhaps pass near me, so that the wind of its presence would tinge my being with some portion of its influence. But none of these actually struck me until one—'twas a bigger star than most—burst into a glorious face more beautiful than sea-born Aphrodite. As it streamed through the sky, the flame of its pace became an aureole of wondrous hair. Nearer, nearer it came; my soul leapt out to meet it. Innocence, god-head, peace, love, gentleness, all infinite rapture were hers. My soul leapt out to meet her. Now! Now! And waves of purest gold streamed through all my being as our lips met in one long passionate kiss.

But, as this endured, it changed. Her lips grew hot—horrible. Beneath her mouth my lips rotted away; unutterable pangs tore asunder my whole being. Suddenly, as a shock, all that soul-shaking vision passes; but it left me trembling. Now, too, all the rapture of joyous expectation began to cloud. The vivid stream of blood in me began to slacken. The faint dawn-blush of the universe tinged its green with rose, with gold—and dull grey patches in the gold. And then I became aware of certain faces behind me. Behind me—however swift I turned, I could only catch the vaguest glimpses of them. But the impression was that of forces too unutterably malignant, menacing. Yet the flood of the exaltation of the vision bore me away, and they were easily forgotten. Until in the full current the star swept upon me from the height, and I recognised the type of face that I had known as Theirs. It passed me, but so close that, fast as it fell, it chilled me horribly. It seemed, too, as if I had moved swiftly to avoid it. And therewith came a sinking fear. Before I had always been stable in a world of change. Now forsooth I too am mobile! the fear shook me horribly.

Then, too, a spasm of remembrance of the evil woman. It was as if her nature had passed into me, become part of me. And I loathed myself. Thus the dreadful war began: that war wherein a man is set against himself—the strife that has no end.

Yet at this very moment a strange, new phenomenon took away my breath—my whole life lost itself therein.

A star grew, brighter than a million stars, and headlong from the vault it fell, rayed with gossamer gold that streamed and filled the whole bright heaven. And as it came to me it loved me—I saw a face of sorrow and strange longing, of hunger for the unattainable mingled with ecstasy for what it had attained. This face drew near to me; and the hands pressed mine, and put them to its lips, and my lips trembled.

Then we kissed, and the vision dissolved into an ecstasy too serene and exquisite to have any object.

As did the other visitor, this too suddenly passed— yet still that star hangs in the vault (so I felt), and will hang ever.

This was a mighty consolation. For now the vision swiftly shifted, and took new forms and lives.

As if the subtle poison of the drug had taken on a new phase.

Not only were the objects of the vision altered, but my point of view began to change.

III

It was no longer expectation of some bliss ineffable that informed the dream. This was remembered, indeed, but with a sneer. Instead of it, dominant, compelling, an apprehension of some horror beyond naming. So terrible seemed the meaning of the vision—that meaning which I had sought so long—that I strove to shut out all reflection upon it, to busy myself with the phenomena themselves.

Yet as I came to myself out of this resolution, it was to see the vulture eyes of one of the Faces, that regarded me, a triumph unholy in its hate against me. I swooned.

Coming to myself again, I strove to regain the lost control. I clung to the tangible, the visible. Yet these gradually deteriorated as time passed. The heaven of gold was almost hidden by angry clouds, the sun, dull, rayless red of dying fire, became a hateful thing.

Anon more shakings of the fear unnameable; anon more visions of corruption, more urgent intimations of the close hostility of those fearful Faces.

Only by stern grip of myself could I shut out this terror—and, once it had entered in, I found strange liability to recurrence.

Yet upon the things visible and tangible, I still gained; their mastery became easy to me. Save only that the action of clasping them as I needed them seemed (it may be) to recall the clutch upon me at the beginning of the vision. With this result, that I became instantly conscious of the fatuity of my state, that the thing I grasped eluded me even because I had succeeded.

Yet so terrible was any inward reflection that I clung still fiercely and more fiercely to the visible gains. How they had changed! Beauty had almost vanished; harmony was clean gone; the one thing desirable yet was a certain rod of iron that hung above me. This I aspired to; this was alike my fear and my desire.

For I feared that it might come whirling through the air and destroy me—unless I could reach up to it—grasp it—make it mine.

So thereunto I strove.

And behold I found myself sitting in a great concourse of monkeys, whose jabber deafened every other sound. Six hundred and sixty-nine there were, and I among them, I one of them.

Yet even so I strove. I aped their cunning, their avarice, their folly; in the end I became head of them.

And now—yes, now at last! the iron rod was in my hand. I raised it to smite—when, lo!

In my struggles I had almost forgotten the Faces. One of them was gazing at me between my eyes.

Yet this time came no merciful swoon to my relief. Conscious of the horror I stood, gasping; while he no longer an elusive phantom but real, positive, awful, shot the dreadful pain, the paralysing fear, through every tiniest path of my whole being.

Then the supreme, the unutterable pang —and blackness—blackness—blackness.

I came to myself. My quiet friend stood smiling by me.

Well!"—his soft voice wooed my sense to life—"how do you like the vision?"

I was still shaking, sweating, shrivelled by the terror of it all.

You were wise." I replied, "did you call the name of it Death!"

Nay!" he answered, with grave sorrow in his eyes, "methinks its name is Life."

Liber A'ash

Gnarled Oak of God! In thy branches is the lightning nested! Above thee hangs the Eyeless Hawk.

Thou art blasted and black! Supremely solitary in that heath of scrub.

Up! The ruddy clouds hang over thee! It is the storm.

There is a flaming gash in the sky.

Up.

Thou art tossed about in the grip of the storm for an eon and an eon and an eon. But thou givest not thy sap; thou fallest not.

Only in the end shalt thou give up thy sap when the great God FIAT is enthroned on the day of Be-With-Us.

For two things are done and a third thing is begun. Isis and Osiris are given over to incest and adultery. Horus leaps up thrice armed from the womb of his mother. Harpocrates his twin is hidden within him. Set is his holy covenant, that he shall display in the great day of MAAT, that is being interpreted the Master of the Temple of A.·.A.·., whose name is Truth.

Now in this is the magical power known.

It is like the oak that hardens itself and bears up against the storm. It is weather-beaten and scarred and confident like a sea-captain.

Also it straineth like a hound in the leash.

It hath pride and great subtlety. Yea, and glee also!

Let the magus act thus in his conjuration.

Let him sit and conjure; let him draw himself together in that forcefulness; let him rise next swollen and straining; let him dash back the hood from his head and fix his basilisk eye upon the sigil of the demon. Then let him sway the force of him to and from like a satyr in silence, until the Word burst from his throat.

Then let him not fall exhausted, although the might have been ten thousandfold the human; but that which floodeth him is the infinite mercy of the Genitor-Genetrix of the Universe, whereof he is the Vessel.

Nor do thou deceive thyself. It is easy to tell the live force from the dead matter. It is no easier to tell the live snake from the dead snake.

Also concerning vows. Be obstinate, and be not obstinate. Understand that the yielding of the Yoni is one with the lengthening of the Lingam. Thou art both these; and thy vow is but the rustling of the wind on Mount Meru.

Now shalt thou adore me who am the Eye and the Tooth, the Goat of the Spirit, the Lord of Creation. I am the Eye in the Triangle, the Silver Star that ye adore.

I am Baphomet, that is the Eightfold Word that shall be equilibrated with the Three.

There is no act or passion that shall not be a hymn in mine honour.

All holy things and all symbolic things shall be my sacraments.

These animals are sacred unto me; the goat, and the duck, and the ass, and the gazelle, the man, the woman, and the child.

All corpses are sacred unto me; they shall not be touched save in mine eucharist. All lonely places are sacred unto me; where one man gathereth himself together in my name, there will I leap forth in the midst of him.

I am the hideous god; and who mastereth me is uglier than I.

Yet I give more than Bacchus and Apollo; my gifts exceed the olive and the horse.

Who worshippeth me must worship me with many rites.

I am concealed with all concealments; when the Most Holy Ancient One is stripped and driven through the marketplace I am still secret and apart.

Whom I love I chastise with many rods.

All things are sacred to me; no thing is sacred from me.

For there is no holiness where I am not.

Fear not when I fall in the fury of the storm; for mine acorns are blown afar by the wind; and verily I shall rise again, and my children about me, so that we shall uplift our forest in Eternity.

Eternity is the storm that covereth me.

I am Existence, the Existence that existeth not save through its own Existence, that is beyond the Existence of Existences, and rooted deeper than the No-Thing-Tree in the Land of No-Thing.

Now therefore thou knowest when I am within thee, when my hood is spread over thy skull, when my might is more than the penned Indus, and resistless as the Giant Glacier.

For as thou art before a lewd woman in Thy nakedness in the bazaar, sucked up by her slyness and smiles, so art thou wholly and no more in part before the symbol of the beloved, though it be but a Pisacha or a Yantra or a Deva.

And in all shalt thou create in Infinite Bliss, and the next link of the Infinite Chain.

This chain reaches from Eternity to Eternity, even in triangles—is not my symbol a triangle?— ever in circles—is not the symbol of the Beloved a circle? Therein is all progress base illusion, for every circle is alike and every triangle alike!

But the progress is progress, and progress is rapture, constant, dazzling, showers of light, waves of dew, flames of the hair of the Great Goddess, flowers of the roses that are about her neck, Amen!

Therefore lift up thyself as I am lifted up. Hold thyself in as I am master to accomplish. At the end, be the end far distant as the stars that lie in the navel of Nuit, do thou slay thyself as I at the end am slain, in the death that is life, in the peace that is the mother of war, in the darkness that holds light in his hand as a harlot that plucks a jewel from her nostrils.

So therefore the beginning is delight, and the End is delight, and delight is in the midst, even as the Indus is water in the cavern of the glacier, and water among the greater hills and the lesser hills and through the ramparts of the hills and through the plains, and water at the mouth thereof when it leaps forth into the mighty sea, yea, into the mighty sea.

[*The Interpretation of this Book will be given to members of the Grade of Dominus Liminis on application, each to his Adeptus.*]

The Dangers of Mysticism

Affectionately Inscribed to Arthur Edward Waite

A curious idea is being sedulously disseminated, and appears to be gaining ground, that mysticism is the "Safe" Path to the Highest, and magic the dangerous Path to the Lowest.

There are several comments to be made on this assertion. One may doubt whether anything worth doing at all is free from danger, and one may wonder what danger can threaten the man whose object is his own utter ruin. One may also smile a little grimly at the integrity of those who try to include all Magic under Black Magic, as is the present trick of the Mystic Militant here on earth.

Now, as one who may claim to a slight acquaintance with the literature of both paths, and to have been honoured by personal exposition from the adepts of both paths, I believe that I may be able to bring them fairly into the balance.

This is the magical theory, that the first departure from the Infinite must be equilibrated and so corrected. So the "great Magician," Mayan, the maker of Illusion, the Creator, must be met in combat. Then "if Satan be divided against Satan, how can his kingdom stand?" Both vanish: the illusion is no more. Mathematically, $1 + (-1) = 0$. And this path is symbolised in the Taro under the figure of the Magus, the card numbered 1, the first departure from 0, but referred to Beth, 2, Mercury, the god of Wisdom, Magic and Truth.

And this Magus has the twofold aspect of the Magician himself and also of the "Great Magician" described in Liber 418.

Now the formula of the mystic is much simpler. Mathematically, it is 1 - 1 = 0. He is like a grain of salt cast into the sea; the process of dissolution is obviously easier than the shock of worlds which the magician contemplates. "Sit down, and feel yourself as dust in the presence of God; nay, as less than dust, as nothing," is the all-sufficient simplicity of his method. Unfortunately, many people cannot do this. And when you urge your inability, the mystic is only too likely to shrug his shoulders and be done with you.

This path is symbolised by the "Fool" of the Tarot, who is alike the Mystic and the Infinite.

But apart from this question, it is by no means certain that the formula is as simple as it seems. How is the mystic to assure himself that "God" is really "God" and not some demon masquerading in His image? We find Gerson sacrificing Huss to his "God"; we find a modern journalist who has done more than dabble in mysticism writing, "This mystic life at its highest is undeniably selfish"; we find another writing like the old lady who ended her criticism of the Universe, "There's only Jock an' me'll be saved; an' I'm no that sure o' Jock"; we find another who at the age of ninety-nine foams at the mouth over an alleged breach of her alleged copyright; we find another so sensitive that the mention of his name by the present writer induces an attack of epileptic mania; if such are really "united with" or "absorbed in" God, what of God?

We are told in Galatians that the fruits of the Spirit are peace, love, joy, long-suffering, gentleness, goodness, faith, meekness, temperance; and somewhere else, "By their fruits ye shall know them."

Of these evil-doers then we must either think that they are dishonest, and have never attained at all, or that they have united themselves with a devil.

Such are "Brethren of the Left Hand Path," described so thoroughly in Liber 418.

Of these the most characteristic sign is their exclusiveness. "We are the men." "Ours is the only Way." "All Buddhists are wicked," the insanity of spiritual pride.

The Magician is not nearly so liable to fall into this fearful mire of pride as the mystic; he is occupied with things outside himself, and can correct his pride. Indeed, he is constantly being corrected by Nature. He, the Great One, cannot run a mile in four minutes! The mystic is solitary and shut up, lacks wholesome combat. We are all schoolboys, and the football field is a perfect prophylactic of swelled head. When the mystic meets an obstacle, he "makes believe" about it. He says it is "only illusion." He has the morphino-maniac's feeling of *bien-etre*, the delusions of the general paralytic. He loses the power of looking any fact in the face; he feeds himself on his own imagination; he persuades himself of his own attainment. If contradicted on the subject, he is cross and spiteful and cattish. If I criticise Mr X, he screams, and tries to injure me behind my back; if I say that Madam Y is not exactly St. Teresa, she writes a book to prove that she is.

Such persons "swollen with wind, and the rank mist they draw, Rot inwardly, and foul contagion spread," as Milton wrote of a less dangerous set of spiritual guides.

For their unhappy followers and imitators, no words of pity suffice. The whole universe is for them but "the glass of their fool's face"; only, unlike Sir Palamedes, they admire it. Moral and spiritual Narcissi, they perish in the waters of illusion. A friend of mine, a solicitor in Naples, has told me strange tales of where such self-adoration ends.

And the subtlety of the devil is shown particularly in the method by which such neophytes are caught by the Black Brothers. There is an exaggerated awe, a solemnity of diction, a vanity of archaic phrases, a false veil of holiness upon the unclean shrine. Stilted affectation masquerades as dignity; a rag-bag of mediaevalism apes profundity; jargon passes for literature; phylacteries increase about the hem of the perfect prig, prude, and Pharisee.

Corollary to this attitude is the lack of all human virtue. The greatest magician, when he acts in his human capacity, acts as a man should. In particular, he has learnt kindheartedness and sympathy. Unselfishness is very often his long suit. Just this the mystic lacks. Trying to absorb the lower planes into the higher, he neglects the lower, a mistake no magician could make.

The Nun Gertrude, when it came to her turn to wash up the dishes, used to explain that she was very sorry, but at that particular moment she was being married, with full choral service, to the Saviour.

Hundreds of mystics shut themselves up completely and for ever. Not only is their wealth-producing capacity lost to society, but so is their love and good-will, and worst of all, so is their example and precept. Christ, at the height of his career, found time to wash the feet of his disciples; any Master who does not do this on every plane is a Black Brother. The Hindus honour no man who becomes "Sannyasi" (nearly our "hermit") until he has faithfully fulfilled all his duties as a man and a citizen. Celibacy is immoral, and the celibate shirks one of the greatest difficulties of the Path.

Beware of all those who shirk the lower difficulties: it's a good bet that they shirk the higher difficulties too.

Of the special dangers of the path there is here no space to write; each student finds at each step temptations reflecting his own special weaknesses. I have therefore dealt solely with the dangers inseparable from the path itself, dangers inherent in its nature. Not for one moment would I ask the weakest to turn back or turn aside from that path, but I would ask even the strongest to apply these correctives: first, the sceptical or scientific attitude, both in outlook and method; second, a healthy life, meaning by that what the athlete and the explorer mean; third, hearty human companionship, and devotion to life, work, and duty.

Let him remember that an ounce of honest pride is better than a ton of false humility, although an ounce of true humility is worth an ounce of honest pride; the man who works has no time to bother with either. And let him remember Christ's statement of the Law "to love God with all thy heart, and thy neighbour as thyself."

The Rosicrucian

I see the centuries wax and wane.
I know their mystery of pain,
    The secrets of the living fire,
The key of life: I live: I reign:
    For I am master of desire.

Silent, I pass amid the folk
Caught in its mesh, slaves to its yoke.
    Silent, unknown, I work and will
Redemption, godhead's master-stroke,
    And breaking of the wands of ill.

No man hath seen beneath my brows
Eternity's exultant house.
    No man hath noted in my brain
The knowledge of my mystic spouse.
    I watch the centuries wax and wane.

Poor, in the kingdom of strong gold,
My power is swift and uncontrolled.
    Simple, amid the maze of lies;
A child, among the cruel old,
    I plot their stealthy destinies.

So patient, in the breathless strife;
So silent, under scourge and knife;
    So tranquil, in the surge of things;

I bring them from the well of Life,
    Love, from celestial water-springs!

From the shrill fountain-head of God
I draw out water with the rod
    Made luminous with light of power.
I seal each eon's period,
    And wait the moment and the hour.

Aloof, alone, unloved, I stand
With love and worship in my hand.
    I commune with the Gods: I wait
Their summons, and I fire the brand.
    I speak their Word : and there is Fate.

I know no happiness, no pain,
No swift emotion, no disdain,
    No pity: but the boundless light
Of the Eternal Love, unslain,
    Flows through me to redeem the night.

Mine is a sad-slow life: but I,
I would not gain release, and die
    A moment ere my task be done.
To falter now were treachery—
    I should not dare to greet the sun!

Yet, in one hour I dare not hope,
The mighty gate of Life may ope,
    And call me upwards to unite

(Even my soul within the scope)
    With That Unutterable Light.

Steady of purpose, girt with Truth,
I pass, in my eternal youth,
    And watch the centuries wax and wane:
Untouched by Time's corroding tooth,
    Silent, immortal, unprofane!

My empire changes not with time.
Men's kingdom's cadent as a rhyme
    Move me as waves that rise and fall.
They are the parts, that crash or climb,
    I only comprehend the All.

I sit, as God must sit; I reign.
Redemption from the threads of pain
    I weave, until the veil be drawn.
I burn the chaff, I glean the grain;
    In silence I await the dawn.

The Law of Liberty

Do what thou wilt shall be the whole of the Law.

I

I am often asked why I begin my letters in this way. No matter whether I am writing to my lady or my butcher, always I begin with these eleven words. Why, how else should I begin? What other greeting could be so glad? Look brother, we are free! Rejoice with me, sister, there is no law beyond Do what thou wilt!

II

I write this for those who have not read our Sacred book, *The Book of the Law*, or for those who, reading it, have somehow failed to understand its perfection. For there are many matters in this Book, and the Glad Tidings are now here, now there, scattered throughout the Book as the Stars are scattered through the field of Night. Rejoice with me, all ye people! At the very head of the Book stands the great charter of our godhead: "Every man and every woman is a star." We are all free, all independent, all shining gloriously, each one a radiant world. Is not that good tidings?

Then comes the first call of the Great Goddess Nuit, Lady of the Starry Heaven who is also Matter in its deepest metaphysical sense, who is the infinite in whom all we live and move and have our being. Hear Her first summons to us men and women: "Come forth, o children, under the stars, & take your fill of love! I am above you and in you. My ecstasy is in yours. My joy is to see your joy." Later She explains the mystery of sorrow: "For I am divided for love's sake, for the chance of union."

"This is the creation of the world, that the pain of division is as nothing, and the joy of dissolution all."

It is shown later how this can be, how death itself is an ecstasy like love, but more intense, the reunion of the soul with its true self.

And what are the conditions of this joy, and peace, and glory? Is ours the gloomy asceticism of the Christian, and the Buddhist, and the Hindu? Are we walking in eternal fear lest some "sin" should cut us off from "grace?" By no means.

"Be goodly therefore: dress ye all in fine apparel; eat rich foods and drink sweet wines and wines that foam! Also, take your fill and will of love as ye will, when, where and with whom ye will! But always unto me."

This is the only point to bear in mind, that every act must be a ritual, an act of worship, a sacrament. Live as the kings and princes, crowned and uncrowned, of this world, have always lived, as masters always live; but let it not be self-indulgence; make your self-indulgence your religion.

When you drink and dance and take delight, you are not being "immoral," you are not "risking your immortal soul"; you are fulfilling the precepts of our holy religion—provided only that you remember to regard your actions in this light. Do not lower yourself and destroy and cheapen your pleasure by leaving out the supreme joy, the consciousness of the Peace that passeth understanding. Do not embrace mere Marian or Melusine; she is Nuit Herself, specially concentrated and incarnated in human form to give you infinite love, to bid you taste even on earth the Elixir of Immortality. "But ecstasy be thine and joy of earth: ever To me! To me!"

Again She speaks: "Love is the law, love under will." Keep pure your highest ideal; strive ever toward it without allowing aught to stop you or turn you aside, even as a star sweeps upon its incalculable and infinite course of glory, and all is Love. The Law of your being becomes Light, Life, Love and Liberty All is peace, all is harmony and beauty, all is joy.

For hear, how gracious is the Goddess; "I give unimaginable joys on earth: certainty, not faith, while in life, upon death; peace unutterable, rest, ecstasy; nor do I demand aught in sacrifice."

Is this not better than the death-in-life of the slaves of Slave-Gods, as they go oppressed by consciousness of "sin," wearily seeking or simulating wearisome and tedious "virtues"?

With such, we who have accepted the Law of Thelema have nothing to do. We have heard the Voice of the Star-Goddess: "I love you! I yearn to you! Pale or purple, veiled or voluptuous, I who am all pleasure and purple, and drunkenness of the innermost sense, desire you. Put on the wings, and arouse the coiled splendour within you: come unto me!" And thus She ends:

"Sing the rapturous love-song unto me! Burn to me perfumes! Wear to me jewels! Drink to me, for I love you! I love you! I am the blue-lidded daughter of Sunset; I am the naked brilliance of the voluptuous night-sky. To me! To me!" And with these words "The Manifestion of Nuit is at an end."

III

In the next chapter of our book is given the word of Hadit, who is the complement of Nuit. He is eternal energy, the Infinite Motion of Thing, the central core of all being. The manifested Universe comes from the marriage of Nuit and Hadit; without this could no thing be. This eternal, this perpetual marriage-feast is then the nature of things themselves; and therefore everything that is, is a crystallization of divine ecstasy.

Hadit tells us of Himself "I am the flame that burns in every heart of man, and in the core of every star." He is then your own inmost divine self; it is you, and not another, who are lost in the constant rapture of the embraces of Infinite Beauty. A little further on He speaks of us:

"We are not for the poor and the sad: the lords of the earth are our kinsfolk."

"Is God to live in a dog? No! but the highest are of us. They shall rejoice, our chosen: who sorroweth is not of us."

"Beauty and strength, leaping laughter and delicious languor, force and fire, are of us." Later, concerning death, He says: "Think not, o king, upon that lie: That Thou Must Die: verily thou shalt not die, but live. Now let it be understood: If the body of the King dissolve, he shall remain in pure ecstasy for ever." When you know that, what is left but delight? And how are we to live meanwhile?

"It is a lie, this folly against self--Be strong, o man! lust, enjoy all things of sense and rapture: fear not that any God shall deny thee for this."

Again and again, in words like these, He sees the expansion and the development of the soul through joy.

Here is the Calendar of our Church: "But ye, o my people, rise up & awake! Let the rituals be rightly performed with joy and beauty!" Remember that all acts of love and pleasure are rituals, must be rituals. "There are rituals of the elements and feasts of the times. A feast for the first night of the Prophet and his Bride! A feast for the three days of the writing of the Book of the Law. A feast for Tahuti and the child of the Prophet—secret, O Prophet! A feast for the Supreme Ritual, and feast for the Equinox of the Gods. A feast for fire and a feast for water; a feast for life and a greater feast for death! A feast every day in your hearts in the joy of my rapture! A feast every night unto Nu, and the pleasure of uttermost delight! Aye! feast! rejoice! there is no dread hereafter. There is the dissolution, and eternal ecstasy in the kisses of Nu." It all depends on you own acceptance of this new law, and you are not asked to believe anything, to accept a string of foolish fables beneath the intellectual level of a Bushman and the moral level of a drug-fiend. All you have to do is to be yourself, to do your will, and to rejoice.

"Dost thou fail? Art thou sorry? Is fear in thine heart?" He says again: "Where I am, these are not." There is much more of the same kind; enough has been quoted already to make all clear. But there is a further injunction. "Wisdom says: be strong! Then canst thou bear more joy. Be not animal; refine thy rapture! If thou drink, drink by the eight and ninety rules of art: if thou love, exceed by delicacy; and if thou do aught joyous, let there be subtlety therein! But exceed! exceed! Strive ever to more! and if thou art truly mine—and doubt it not, an if thou art ever joyous!—death is the crown of all."

Lift yourselves up, my brothers and sisters of the earth! Put beneath your feet all fears, all qualms, all hesitancies! Lift yourselves up! Come forth, free and joyous, by night and day, to do your will; for "There is no law beyond Do what thou wilt." Lift yourselves up! Walk forth with us in Light and Life and Love and Liberty, taking our pleasure as Kings and Queens in Heaven and on Earth.

The sun is arisen; the spectre of the ages has been put to flight. "The word of Sin is Restriction," or as it has been otherwise said on this text: That is Sin, to hold thine holy spirit in!

Go on, go on in thy might; and let no man make thee afraid.

Love is the law, love under will.

www.ingramcontent.com/pod-product-compliance
Lightning Source LLC
Chambersburg PA
CBHW032125090426
42743CB00007B/466